THE
SPIDER-MAN®
HANDBOOK

A LITTLE COMMON SPIDER-SENSE

Even though the words *handbook* and *manual* appear in its title, this book is actually a work of fiction. Brilliant, masterfully crafted fiction, yes—but fiction nonetheless. And even though the author has provided the most accurate, real-world information available, he's done so purely for the purpose of entertaining you, the captivated reader.

Yes, Spider-Man rules. Yes, it would be completely awesome to be him. But (brace yourselves) he's only make-believe. Attempting the things outlined in this book could land you in *real* jail or lead to *real* injury, insanity, death—even bankruptcy (do you have any idea how expensive web fluid is?). In other words, don't try this at home. Any of it. Get a spider bite? Go to the hospital. See a thug with a gun? Call the police. Guy with a goblin mask starts throwing exploding pumpkins at you? Run for your life.

Just to show you how serious we are about this, allow us to drop some legalese on you:

And remember, whatever you do, don't marry an actress. That's just suicide.

THE
SPIDER-MAN®
HANDBOOK

THE ULTIMATE
TRAINING MANUAL

By Seth Grahame-Smith
Foreword by Stan Lee
Illustrations by Carlo Barberi

QUIRK BOOKS
PHILADELPHIA

Published by Quirk Productions, Inc.

MARVEL, Spider-Man, and all related characters, names, and likenesses thereof are trademarks of Marvel Characters, Inc., and are used with permission.

www.marvel.com

This handbook was produced under license from Marvel Characters, Inc.

Library of Congress Cataloging in Publication Number: 2006902592

ISBN-10: 1-59474-125-5
ISBN-13: 978-1-59474-125-8

Printed in Singapore

Typeset in Antique Olive, Futura, and Gill Sans

Designed and colored by Michael Rogalski
Production management by Chris Veneziale

Distributed in North America by Chronicle Books
85 Second Street
San Francisco, CA 94105

10 9 8 7 6 5 4 3 2 1

Quirk Books
215 Church Street
Philadelphia, PA 19106
www.quirkbooks.com

Contents

FOREWORD

I don't blame you!

I don't blame you for wanting to be like Spider-Man. Who wouldn't want to experience the fun and excitement of the web-swinger's life? Who wouldn't want to be a hero to millions of fans and have his life story chronicled in movies, books, video games, television, and DVDs?

Now, thanks to this great book, you'll have that chance—a chance to be more like Spider-Man than you ever dreamed possible!

Have you ever wondered why so many people, all over the world, identify with Peter Parker? I'm guessing it's because he isn't perfect. He has money problems, just like you and me; hang-ups and insecurities, just like you and me; and he's not always sure he's doing the right thing, just like—uh huh, you guessed it. Pretty easy to relate to a guy who's not that different from you, right?

Of course, he can go web-swinging over the city, free and unfettered, fast as the wind. Plus, he can crawl up the side of a building and shoot a web that's bigger and stronger than any the mightiest spider can spin. But those aren't the things that make him a hero. Without certain all-important qualities, he'd just be another colorful circus performer.

What are those important qualities? You'll find them described in detail in this really helpful book while you're learning how to maintain a secret identity, how to create a costume, even how to swing from building to building—in short, everything a would-be web-swinger needs to know. And here's possibly the most important fact: We all have the power to perform heroic acts in our own daily lives, which is why you yourself have the chance to be a super hero.

However, just one word of warning. If, after reading this book, you've succeeded in mastering the art and the skills of super-hero-dom, be sure to keep your true identity secret—because there's just a chance that Spider-Man may not like the competition!

Excelsior!
Stan Lee

INTRODUCTION

Peter Parker was nothing special—just another kid trying to make it out of high school in one piece. And things weren't looking good. After all, he was a puny, four-eyed wallflower who lived with his cash-strapped aunt and uncle. No money? No muscles? No mojo? In high school terms, that's a trifecta of unpopularity. And to make matters worse, he was smart. *Really* smart. Oh, the humanity!

Chances are, Pete would've served out the remainder of his Midtown High sentence in relative obscurity—popping up for the occasional science club meeting and enduring semiregular hazing from the varsity squad. But we'll never know, because fate (in the guise of Stan Lee and Steve Ditko) had other ideas for the lad. Ideas they famously injected through the fangs of a radioactive spider. Since 1963, that little bug bite has spawned tons of comic books, multiple television series, record-breaking movies, several video games, and who knows how many millions of loyal fans around the world.

Why?

What is it about the web-slinger that we love? Is it the red and blue (or more recently black) tights? The Tarzanlike way he traverses lower Manhattan? The sculpted abs?

Nah.

It's the guy *under* the mask. The social outcast who never in his wildest dreams thought he'd be a super hero. The quiet kid who pines for the unattainable homecoming queen, struggles to pay the bills, and takes abuse from his boss (and does it all with a wicked sense of humor). He's not a melo-dramatic billionaire. He's not a goody two-shoes from outer space. He's just your friendly neighborhood kind of guy. He's one of *us*. That's why we root him on—and why Spider-Man is the ultimate role model for aspiring super heroes.

But "aspiring" to be Spider-Man isn't enough. It takes training, discipline, and knowledge. (Well, that and genetic mutation, but let's not split hairs.) The point is, who taught Peter Parker how to escape from an enemy's secret headquarters? Who taught him the dos and don'ts of costume design? Where did he buy the schematics for a spider-shaped tracking device? The answer to each of those rhetorical questions is "nobody." Well, except for the last one, which I guess would be "nowhere."

No, Pete had to learn all of his spider-lessons through trial and (more often) error. Lucky for you, fearless reader, this book is designed to spare you the bumps and bruises of the Spider-Man learning curve—a curve fraught with villainous geniuses, gun-wielding thugs, venomous robot babies, and past-due notices. The following pages will teach you how to defeat them all. They'll teach you how to prepare your body and mind for the task of keeping the world safe from evil. They'll even teach you how to keep your marriage together, if you're into that sort of thing.

So as you embark on your new crime-fighting career, remember two things: First, the strength of your character is more important than the strength of your punches (although it never hurts to pack a solid right hook). And second, in the words of Uncle Ben, "With great power comes great responsibility."

Now get out there and do some good.

Chapter 1

The Basics

"True knowledge exists in knowing that you know nothing."
—Socrates

Spidey makes it look easy. But being a web-slinging, wall-crawling, fear-striking super hero takes practice. You'll need a combination of physical ability, mental fortitude, and good old-fashioned smarts to pull it off. A background in fashion design wouldn't hurt, either.

How to Treat
a Radioactive Spider Bite

Bad? A venomous spider sinks its fangs into you. Worse? Its venom has a half-life of 5,000 years. There are about 37,000 identified species of spider in the world, and scientists estimate that another 150,000 have yet to be identified. So is it *that* hard to believe that one of those undiscovered species might be radioactive? Peter Parker was lucky enough to get tagged by a spider whose venom somehow mutated his biochemistry and gave him superpowers (without causing him to grow six extra legs, making his hair fall out, or sending him to the big web in the sky). However, it's doubtful the combined effects of spider venom and radiation poisoning would provide you with an equally enriching experience. If you should happen to fall prey to an arachnid with nuclear chompers, you'll have to keep your wits to keep your life.

Step 1: Capture the spider.
It's imperative that you trap the spider immediately, dead or alive. If you're feeling humane, place a clear plastic container over the critter, and then seal it with a lid (be sure to punch a few holes for air). But if there's any chance of the spider escaping—and remember, they can be fast—squash the little bugger with your shoe.

Step 2: Determine the level of radiation exposure.
The clock is ticking, so hurry up and get your hands on a Geiger counter (if you're anything like Peter, you'll have one lying around somewhere) and measure the spider's level of radioactivity. This will let you (and your doctor) know what kind of reaction to expect. Human exposure to radiation is measured in units called sieverts, which can be interpreted in the following manner:

- $1/2$ to 2 sieverts: You can expect headaches, fatigue, and nausea—nothing you wouldn't experience after a meeting with J. J. Jameson.

- 2 to 3 sieverts: Your chance of death is 35 percent, and you can add hair loss, vomiting, and other gastrointestinal goodies to your list of symptoms.

- 3 to 4 sieverts: You have a 50/50 chance of survival, and you'll get to discover the joys of internal bleeding.

- Anything greater than 4 sieverts: It's highly recommended that you put this book down and set your affairs in order.

Step 3: Don't do anything stupid.
Like applying a tourniquet or having a friend try to suck the venom out, for example. By the time you manage to tie off the affected limb, the radioactive venom will have already spread to other parts of your body, and if applied incorrectly, a tourniquet can actually end up costing you an arm or a leg—literally. Likewise, having a friend suck the venom out won't do you any good. If anything, it'll spread the poison to *them*.

Step 4: Sterilize the wound.
This may seem trivial, but it could mean the difference between life and death—especially since your immune system is about to take a little vacation. Start by thoroughly cleaning the bite with soap and water. Next, apply a liberal amount of antibiotic ointment. It's bad enough that you've just been snacked on by an eight-legged nuclear reactor—don't make things worse by getting an infection.

Step 5: Get professional help.
You may be a super hero, but this is no time for heroics. You need a doctor, and you need one fast. Since most spiders use venom to immobilize their prey, it's likely that you'll experience severe muscle cramping, respiratory difficulty, even partial paralysis in the first one to two hours. Translation: Get to an emergency room—and don't get there by web-slinging from building to building, or you're likely to wind up pancaked on Fifth Avenue.

- Treating the spider's venom.
  Doctors have a few different weapons to counter the effects of spider venom. Depending on the severity of the symptoms, corticosteroids (cortisone and similar drugs) may be used to relieve inflammation and keep your airway open. In some cases, antivenins—drugs made with horse, rabbit, or other animal antibodies—will be administered. If treated with antivenins in the first four to five hours, some "fatal" doses can be turned into "near fatal" doses. But even the

If bitten by a radioactive spider, you must seek professional help immediately.

Trap the spider in a clear plastic container. Seal it and punch some holes for air.

most severe black widow bite usually isn't enough to kill a healthy adult. What you really have to worry about is that pesky radiation.

- Treating the radiation poisoning.
  The good news: Assuming you've received a fairly mild level of exposure (say, one to two sieverts), you'll probably live. The bad news: You're going to suffer some pretty unpleasant side effects (think Linda Blair in *The Exorcist*), and there's almost nothing your doctors can do about it. There are experimental drugs that show promise for reversing the effects of radiation exposure, but for now, the best you can hope for is a little help while your body heals itself. Antinausea drugs and heavy-duty painkillers can make your inevitable discomfort a little more comfortable.

Step 6: Get yourself checked regularly.
Even after the immediate symptoms fade away, you're still in the woods. Some secondary effects of radiation exposure can take 10 to 15 years to manifest themselves. These include heightened risk of cataracts, certain cancers (like leukemia), and genetic defects that can be passed on to your offspring. So it behooves you to stay in touch with your physician for regular check-ups. Of course, since you're a crime fighter and all, that's probably a good idea anyway.

How to Crawl up a Wall

Spider-Man's hands and feet can stick to any solid surface. This power allows him to scale buildings and scurry across ceilings with ease—pretty handy when you're trying to avoid gunfire or eavesdrop on a dastardly conversation. Real insects accomplish this feat with microscopic hairs that hook into the imperfections found on most surfaces, or with glands that secrete sticky fluid from their appendages. But how does Spider-Man do it? The truth is, no one knows for sure. Peter Parker himself has often cogitated about the mechanics of his wall-crawling ways but hasn't come up with anything conclusive. What he *does* know is this: 1) He only clings when he wants to (otherwise he'd be The Amazing Adhesive-Man, and his relationship with Mary Jane would enter a new realm of complexity), and 2) the bond is incredibly strong. Spidey's been known to take chunks of concrete along when a foe rips him off a building. However, since you don't have the luxury of microscopic fur or naturally sticky fingertips, you'll need to find a more practical method of making like a spider.

Step 1: Choose your route wisely.
A hostage (let's say Betty Brant) is being held on an upper floor of an office tower. Goons are stationed at every entrance, making a direct assault too dangerous. The only option? Scale the building and enter through a window. First, remove any notions of suction cups from your head: They only work on extremely smooth surfaces, and they'll just slow you down. Strength, determination, and a few rock-climbing basics are the quickest way to the top—but before you start using your arms and legs, use your eyes to scout the best route. Look for anything that might aid your ascent—ledges, cracks, or other holds.

Step 2: Prepare to climb.
Once you've mapped out your path, take a few moments to stretch. It may sound silly (what with Betty in mortal peril and all), but freehand climbing is extremely strenuous—and you can't risk cramping up ten stories above street level. Next, make sure your hands are sweat-free. Rubbing some rock-climbing chalk between

them is best, but dry soil will work in a pinch. It's also recommended that you tuck in your shoelaces, lest you accidentally step on one and lose your footing. Last but not least, take a quick inventory of your crime-fighting gear and ditch anything that isn't absolutely necessary. Less freight means less weight, and that means less strain on your puny mortal muscles.

> Every part of Spider-Man's body has the same amount of clinging power—not just his hands and feet. That means he can carry an unconscious victim on his back while keeping both arms and legs free to scurry to safety. It also means you'll never see Peter Parker's hat blow off on a windy day.

Step 3: Get a grip and start your ascent.

Start by finding your first hold. Depending on what you can reach from ground level, there are two techniques that might come in handy:

- Pinching: For anchoring to horizontal cracks—say, between bricks. Straighten your fingers and extend your thumb so it's at a 90 degree angle from your index finger (as if you were going to shake someone's hand). Next, rotate your hand so your palm is facing the ground. Dig your fingers in to get a solid grip, and then close your thumb to "pinch" the hold.

- Jamming: For anchoring to vertical cracks. Extend your hand as above and insert your fingers, making sure you thumb is pointing toward the ground. Next, rotate your hand clockwise so your fingers "jam" inside the tight space. Jamming allows you to take strain off your biceps while you hang in place and plot your next move.

Once you have a firm grip with one or both hands, find a foothold and push yourself up the wall with your legs. The goal is to use your biceps as little as possible. Don't pull up with your arms unless it's absolutely necessary! And rather than climb with your toes, it's better to keep the insides of your feet against the wall—more surface area equals better grip.

Step 4: Maintain a low profile.

As you climb, keep your torso pressed against the building. This keeps your center of gravity closer to the wall and transfers more weight to your legs (which are much stronger than your arms). Likewise, whenever you come to rest, make sure your arms are fully extended. It's much easier to hang in place than hold position in mid pull-up.

Step 5: Visualize your next move.

Time may be of the essence, but moving too quickly can work against you. When climbing, your mind is just as crucial as your might—and you should give both ample rest. Follow every move with a few seconds of downtime. While your muscles recharge, look around for the next crack, or ledge, or foothold. Imagine yourself grabbing on and transferring your weight. Imagine which muscles you'll use and in which order. Imagine yourself taking the stairs next time.

Step 6: Climb one by one.

When you're rested and ready to continue up the wall, start by moving your hands into position one at a time. Once you've got a solid grip, lift your legs into position—again, one at a time. (This reduces the amount of weight your arms have to support). Keep repeating this sequence until you've reached the desired floor, and then proceed with your daring rescue.

Oh, and no peeping in people's windows. "With great power comes great responsibility," remember?

Peter determines the best route before climbing, looking for ledges, cracks, and other holds.

He pinches the bricks to anchor himself on horizontal cracks . . .

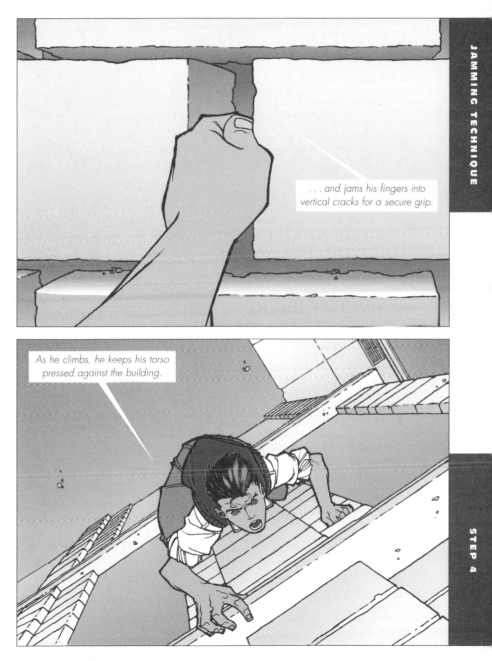

... and jams his fingers into vertical cracks for a secure grip.

As he climbs, he keeps his torso pressed against the building.

How to Design and Build a Costume

Peter Parker's first costume wasn't designed with crime fighting in mind (perhaps that explains the less-than-stealthy choices of bright red and blue). At first, the socially awkward science major saw his new powers as a ticket to fame, fortune, and glory. After proving his mettle in a wrestling contest, Peter hooked up with a television producer who invited him to perform on *The Ed Sullivan Show*. Before the taping, Peter created the prototype of the skintight costume we know and love today. Of course, that was before he unwittingly allowed Uncle Ben's killer to slip through his fingers, and . . . well, you know the rest. In a way, your costume is your greatest superpower. It can instill fear, amplify your abilities, and even save your life. It also protects your secret identity—and by extension, the identities of your loved ones. Anyone considering a career in crime fighting would be wise to master the art of the sewing machine, because real super heroes spend as much time stitching as on vigilante work.

Choose your concept carefully. Peter didn't have to rack his considerable brain to come up with a super hero concept. After all, when you're a *man* with the powers of a *spider*, "Spider-Man" kind of seems like the prudent choice. The motif also worked because, generally speaking, people are terrified of the eight-legged critters. Parker built on that natural fear by designing a costume with webs (the original even had webbed netting between the arms and torso), unrevealing bug eyes, and a big spider on the chest. Whatever your alter ego turns out to be, remember that a good costume (like Spidey's) works on multiple levels:

• It clearly conveys your super-identity: For instance, there's no ambiguity in Captain America's costume. You're not going to look at a guy with red, white, and blue tights, a starred shield, a winged mask, and a giant A on his costume and mistake him for Captain Lithuania.

• It's intimidating: That's assuming you've picked an intimidating super hero concept to begin with (if your heart's set on "Baby Panda–Man," you may want to reconsider). Spider-Man's costume benefits from all the creepy features of arachnids—the sticky webs, the inhuman eyes, and the eight legs emblazoned on his chest. Likewise, your outfit should focus on the frightening side of whatever theme you've chosen. For instance, if it's an eagle, play up the pointed beak, piercing eyes, and razor-sharp talons.

- It's functional: After all, this isn't a fashion show. Ultimately, your costume is a tool to aid in the fight against injustice—a line of defense protecting your body and your anonymity. Some super heroes (without naming names) look more like club-goers than crime fighters.

Choose materials that are lightweight, durable, comfortable, and discreet. There's a reason you don't see Spider-Man traipsing around in wool or denim. Like the web-slinger's, your duds shouldn't be obtrusive. Skintight costumes are a must for three reasons:

- Strike a pose: You've worked hard for those ripped pecs and rock-hard quads. Why not show them off? If anything, it'll make your foes think twice about taking you on.

- Comfort and discretion: Your costume needs to be tight enough to hide under your street clothes—and breathable enough to keep you comfortable. (Wearing extra layers is fine during colder months, but come summer, you'll be sweating like a politician at a press conference). Go with materials that allow the skin to breathe when it's warm but retain body heat when it's cool, such as the synthetic fabrics used in modern sporting undergarments.

- Tactical advantage: Skintight costumes offer your opponents less to grab on to during a fight and allow you full freedom of movement.

The one drawback of a skintight outfit is strength. There isn't much room for armor in a leotard, and you'll still be vulnerable to knives and bullets (all the more reason to keep honing your Spider-Sense and combat skills). That's not to say you'll be totally defenseless. Once your suit is finished, have it treated with fireproofing chemicals for added protection. And if the occasion calls for a little something extra, you can always follow in Spider-Man's steps: He's been known to make

The Basics

some extensive modifications to the ol' red and blue (see "The Many Looks of Spider-Man," page 27).

▓▓◖◗▓▓ Keep your sleeves and pant legs short.

Imagine: You're sitting in Jameson's office, trying to dodge flecks of spit as he rants about the "crap you call photography," when suddenly—he stops, his gaze locked on your arm. The cigar falls out of his mouth, and the hairs on the back of your neck stand up as you realize what he's fixated on. Your shirt sleeve has come undone, revealing the arm of your Spider-Suit. It's a very real, very avoidable catastrophe. Your costume's sleeves should end about halfway down your forearm, and your tights should extend no farther than halfway down your calves.

▓▓◖◗▓▓ Gloves, boots, and masks should be especially light.

Spider-Man's hands and feet are covered in extra-thin material to keep his suit from interfering with those mysterious wall-clinging abilities. But that's not the only reason that the appendages of his outfit are considerably lighter. When he's in Peter Parker mode, his gloves, boots, and mask need to stay tucked away without creating unsightly bulges or impeding normal movements. Besides easy storage, having a mask made from lighter fabric allows air to pass through more freely (you may be a super hero, but you still have to breathe).

▓▓◖◗▓▓ Cover your body completely.

One of the things that makes Spider-Man so unique is the fact that he's the only major super hero who doesn't leave a single piece of skin exposed. And though it's not a commonly used costume template, it's one you might want to consider borrowing for a couple of reasons:

• Total anonymity: Once that suit is on, there's no telling who's wearing it. It's impossible for an observer to know Spider-Man's skin or hair color, whether or not he has any tattoos, or what his facial characteristics are. And by shielding his eyes, he not only covers a recognizable feature, he prevents his enemies from gaining even the slightest insight into his thinking.

• The "inhuman" factor: We humans tend to look for certain things when we interact with others: eye contact, mouth movement, facial expressions. We understand them. They make us comfortable. Conversely, there's something inherently uncomfortable about something that doesn't have a face. Something sinister and unpredictable (like the creatures in the *Alien* films).

■◆■ Design a place to store essential tools.

A compartmentalized belt or vest is a must. Just as tight-fitting costumes leave little room for armor (and little to the imagination), they also fall short in the pockets department, and a super hero needs somewhere to carry his or her gadgets. Spider-Man wears a thin storage belt under his tights to hold essentials like web fluid cartridges, spider-tracers, and, of course, a miniature camera to help Peter pay the rent. As with the rest of your costume, make sure to trim any extra weight from your accessory belt or vest and have it chemically fireproofed.

If you're forced to make a quick costume change, there's always the question of where to put your street clothes. When Spidey needs to ditch his civvies, he usually webs them up in a ball and sticks them out of sight, carries them around in a sort of "web-knapsack," or ditches them altogether.

■◆■ Avoid unnecessary accessories.

Capes weigh you down, snag loose nails when you're chasing crooks, give adversaries an advantage in hand-to-hand combat, and worst of all track dirt and dust indoors. Sure, they're flashy and dramatic, but who cares about style when you're getting manhandled up and down Lower Manhattan? Leave the capes to vampires and seventies rock stars.

And while you're at it, avoid anything that adds unnecessary weight or grab points to your costume. Common super hero faux pas include heavy metal arm- and wristbands, unwieldy helmets, and long hair.

We usually think of Spidey in his familiar reds and blues. But depending on the situation (or the century), he might sport an alternate costume:

Underarm Webbing
Peter's early Spider-Man costumes featured nylon webbing that stretched from his waist to his elbows (and later, all the way to his wrists). While it didn't seem to limit his mobility, this decorative touch probably looked strange when hidden under his civilian clothes.

Spider-Armor
When Spidey was gearing up for a climactic battle against Blood Rose, Gauntlet, and the nefarious New Enforcers, he constructed a Spider-Suit covered in heavy armored plates. Though they looked like metal, the plates were actually made from a modified web formula.

The Black Costume
Probably the most recognized look after the reds and blues, Spider-Man first picked up his black duds in 1984. This "costume" actually turned out to be a living alien symbiote that could read Peter's thoughts, generate endless webbing, and morph into street clothes. Eventually, Spidey ditched the alien, which went in search of a new host (see "Know Your Enemy: Venom," page 150).

Spider-Man 2099
The New York of the future has its very own Spider-Man, Miguel O'Hara, whose suit includes a cape made of "lite byte," a synthetic material that helps him glide through the air.

Die Spinne
Peter can't have his costume with him 24 hours a day, and sometimes he's forced to improvise when duty calls. In a pinch, he's substituted everything from hooded sweatshirts to brown paper bags. Once, when trouble arose on a trip to Germany, he hurried to a nearby costume shop, where the owner just happened to have a replica in stock. Granted, it had the words *Die Spinne* ("The Spider") on the back, but beggars can't be choosers.

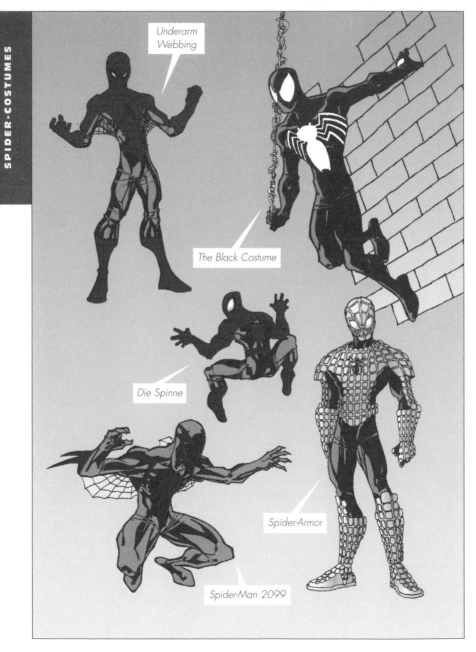

Underarm Webbing

The Black Costume

Die Spinne

Spider-Armor

Spider-Man 2099

How to Build a Web-Shooter

Without his trusty web-shooters, Spider-Man would be nothing but an incredibly strong, sharp-witted guy in tights. Not bad, but not the friendly neighborhood wall-crawler we know and love. A webless Spider-Man would be reduced to handcuffing ne'er-do-wells. He'd have to pause and set up a tripod to capture snaps for the *Daily Bugle*. Worse yet, if trouble broke out on the other side of the city, he'd be forced to hail a cab or catch the subway. A crime fighter at the mercy of crosstown traffic? A sorry sight indeed. The web sets Spider-Man apart, giving him the freedom to quickly and gracefully navigate New York and allowing him to stop runaway subway cars and catch free-falling innocents—and best of all, it's the web that makes him a stand-out in the super hero crowd. Constructing this important accessory is the first step in becoming as effective and distinctive as the worldwide web-slinger himself.

Step 1: Engineer a highly adhesive, shear-thinning, air-hardening/dissolving, nontoxic, fire-resistant polymer with three times the tensile strength of steel. Anyone who passed high school chemistry should have little or no trouble with this step. Just make sure your concoction lives up to the following performance specs:

- It's extremely strong: When you're using it to swing dozens of stories above the street, keep a school bus from teetering over a cliff, or hold an archvillain at bay, you want your web to be nothing short of indestructible. Pound for pound, Spider-Man's sticky strands have three times the tensile strength of galvanized steel. That means 1/8 inch (3.2 mm) of web will support up to 6,000 pounds (2,722 kg)!

- It's a shear-thinning liquid: *Shear thinning* or *shear thickening* refer to the effects of a shearing force (say, being forced through a nozzle at high speed) on a fluid's viscosity. Spidey's fluid is shear thinning—stored in a near-solid state inside his web cartridges until it passes through the shooters' nozzles.

- It hardens, then dissolves upon contact with air: Being a super hero isn't always about roundhouse kicks and daring escapes; sometimes it's just about being a good neighbor. The always-conscientious Peter designed his webs to turn into powder 60 minutes after coming into contact with air. Otherwise, given all the web-slinging Spider-Man does, Manhattan would start looking like the world's biggest haunted house.

- **It's nontoxic:** It wouldn't do much good to save Mary Jane from plummeting to her death only to have her die of poisoning an hour later. Same goes for any criminals you might ensnare (you're a crime fighter, not a murderer). And since your web turns to powder, there's also a risk of polluting the city's air and water.

- **It's fire resistant:** Spidey's been known to whip up a web shield when battling fire-wielding foes, and with good reason: A typical web can withstand temperatures in excess of 1,000 degrees Fahrenheit (538°C). And if he has enough warning, he can switch to a special web fluid that handles up to ten times that temperature.

- **It's highly adhesive:** Your web is only as good as the strength of its bond. Spider-Man's web may be tougher than steel, but that wouldn't matter without its ability to form an instant, virtually unbreakable bond with almost any surface.

Piece of cake, right?

Step 2: Store the polymer with propellant in tiny cartridges.
Once you've perfected a web fluid formula, you'll need a vessel to carry it in. Peter uses refillable metal cartridges, each about the size of a small cell phone battery. A single cartridge typically yields about 1,000 yards (914 m) of webbing, depending on the thickness of the stream (see step 4). This kind of efficiency is possible because the fluid is stored in a near-solid state under tremendous pressure with a propellant. Propellants are usually the vapor of a nonflammable liquid that has a boiling point below room temperature. In aerosol cans, the most common are hydrocarbons (which have the drawback of being flammable) and nitrous oxide or "laughing gas" (which isn't flammable, but may render you incapable of performing your spider-duties).

Step 3: Construct spinneret nozzles.
Spider-Man's web shooters don't fire one solid "string" of material. In fact, a close-up of his webbing would reveal smaller strands that have been joined

together like rope. The advantage is obvious—it's much, much stronger—but getting it that way requires some ingenuity. Peter found his answer in a spinneret nozzle. A "spinneret" (named for the spider organ that excretes silk) is similar to a shower head or pasta press in that it has a collection of holes through which a substance is compressed, creating thin strands of material or streams of liquid. When the web fluid is forced through the spinnerets, what had been a near solid is sheared into multiple streams. And since this is a shear-thinning liquid, the act of compressing it through the spinneret returns the web substance to its fluid state. But it doesn't stay that way for long: The instant the web fluid exits the nozzle and hits the air, it begins to expand and harden. And by the time it's a few feet from Spider-Man's wrist, it's a solid (albeit a very sticky, stretchy one).

Step 4: Make the nozzles adjustable so the webbing's consistency can be altered. The right tool for the right job. Spider-Man's web shooters have nozzles of varying shapes and thicknesses, allowing him to change the type of web he dispenses. For getting around the city, he uses a relatively thin strand to conserve fluid. However, if he's trying to keep a chunk of skyscraper from crashing onto innocent bystanders, he can instantly increase the web's thickness. When the situation calls for something a bit more delicate (say, mounting a camera or balling up street clothes), the webbing can be sprayed as a fine mist. At the other end of the spectrum, when Spidey *really* wants someone or something to stay put, he can dispense the web fluid as an ultra-sticky paste.

Step 5: Build wrist-mounted housings for the nozzles. The housings (or "wristlets") need to be durable without being heavy, tight without being constrictive, and small enough to stay concealed beneath your costume—but not so small that they run the risk of buckling under pressure (Spider-Man's are slightly wider than a sweatband). Start by taking plaster casts of each wrist and using them to make molds. Next, pour molten metal into the molds (for best results, use a metal with a high strength to weight ratio, such as a titanium alloy). Once the metal has cooled, grind down any rough edges and weld the spinneret nozzles to the underside of the housing. For added comfort and slip-proofing, you may also want to consider lining the insides of each wristlet with rubber cushioning.

Step 6: Add a trigger mechanism.
Like the gunslingers of the Old West, web-slingers need to be quick on the draw. Spider-Man's trigger extends from just beneath the spinneret nozzle to the top of his palm, where it widens into a small disk. To fire, he simply taps the disk twice (in rapid succession) with his middle and ring fingers. This double-tap feature helps avoid dangerous (and let's face it, Freudian) misfires. The longer the second tap lasts, the thicker the strand.

Step 7: Keep plenty of spare cartridges on hand.
Each of Spider-Man's web-shooters holds ten cartridges: one attached to the nozzle and nine spares lining the outside of the wristlets. The efficiency-minded Peter Parker even created a mechanism that automatically changes cartridges when one runs dry! You'd think that 20 spares would be enough, but just to be on the safe side, Spidey also wears a belt that holds an additional 30 cartridges.

THE WONDERFUL WORLD OF WEBBING

Some sculptors work in clay, others in stone. Spider-Man's medium of choice? Web fluid. Over the years, he's become a virtuoso of this versatile goo, spinning just about anything he can imagine, from the obvious (parachutes and trampolines) to the bizarre (airtight domes). He's even used his web to make a functional aircraft (see "How to Make and Fly a Web Hang Glider," page 62). And you thought duct tape had a million uses.

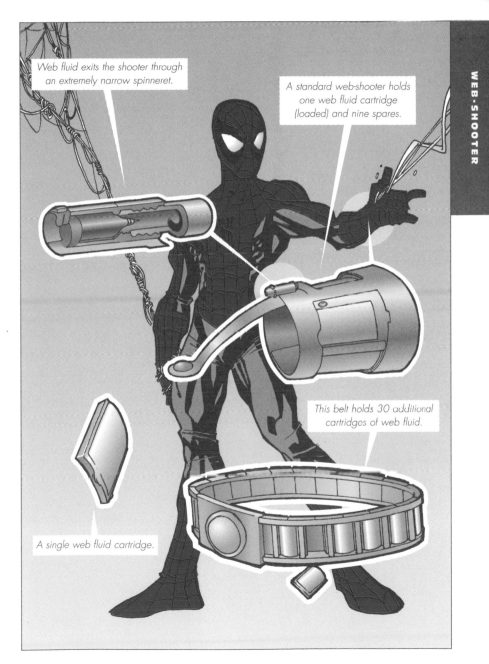

Web fluid exits the shooter through an extremely narrow spinneret.

A standard web-shooter holds one web fluid cartridge (loaded) and nine spares.

This belt holds 30 additional cartridges of web fluid.

A single web fluid cartridge.

How to Build a Web-Shooter 33

How to Swing from Building to Building

When he needs to get somewhere in a hurry, Spider-Man simply points his web-shooters skyward and uses the tall buildings of Manhattan as his personal taxicab. Whether speeding across the city, landing on top of a getaway car, or snatching a little girl from the clutches of death, Spidey makes it all look effortless. But rest assured, it isn't. There's a reason gymnasts start training while they're in diapers, and there's a reason giant ropes never caught on as a form of mass transit. It's dangerous, it's difficult, and it's expensive (you think web fluid grows on trees?). However, short of flying, it's also the fastest way to navigate New York. So if you're serious about donning the red and blue, you'd better pay attention—or you might end up as a permanent addition to the skyline.

Step 1:   Get yourself some energy.

Spidey's often depicted shooting webs from ground level and pulling himself into full swing from a standstill. It may work in comic books, but unless you've got an old pair of rocket boots lying around, you'll have to deal with the physics of the real world. Before you can make like a monkey, you need one of two things: either potential or kinetic energy.

- Kinetic energy: The energy of an object in motion—say, a subway car that you happen to be fighting atop. If you shoot a web onto a nearby building, the train's speed (energy) will be transferred to you, allowing you to swing away.

- Potential energy: The energy stored in an object—say, you standing on the ledge of a tall building. If you shoot a web onto a lower portion of an adjacent building, the potential energy is the difference in height (gravity), plus your own weight. Once you leap, all that stored energy will accelerate your body, and off you'll go.

Step 2:   Shoot your first anchor, grab the web, and launch.

Take aim and fire off a strand, being sure to pick a strong anchor point such as a concrete building or steel bridge. Avoid anchoring to flagpoles, windows, or billboards if possible, since these could buckle or break under the tremendous force you're about to apply (don't lose any sleep over your web, though—it's three times stronger than steel). After firing, grab onto the end of the strand and prepare to release. If you're on a moving platform, it's as easy as pulling yourself upward and lifting your feet into the air. From a stationary platform, lean back slightly and jump one or two feet (30–60 cm) in the air, then allow yourself to fall down into the arc of your swing.

 Leaning forward and simply "falling into it" won't work. Your legs will inevitably flail, robbing your swing of some of the energy it needs to lift you up again.

Step 3: Keep your knees close to your chest and hold on tight.
On the way down, keep your body tucked as tightly as possible. This is important for two reasons: One, because of the aforementioned problem of flailing legs. Two, because it makes your body considerably more aerodynamic. As you descend, centrifugal force will make your body feel heavier and heavier, so it's vital that you maintain a firm grasp on the web.

Step 4: Kick your feet forward at the bottom of the swing.
If you need an example of this technique, simply observe the swing set at your local playground. When a child wants to swing forward (upward), she'll extend her legs and straighten her body. Likewise, as you near the bottom of your arc, kick your feet uniformly forward and straighten your body as much as possible (with any luck, this will happen instinctively). This maneuver not only preserves the energy you built up on the way down, it puts you in perfect position for the next two steps.

Step 5: Shoot your second anchor during the ascent.
You're gaining altitude, legs fully extended. Now, using your free web-shooter, take aim and fire a strand at the next anchor point. Do this as early in the ascent as possible (if you miss, you'll need time to get off a second shot). Assuming your aim is true, grab hold of the second strand and get ready to make the swap.

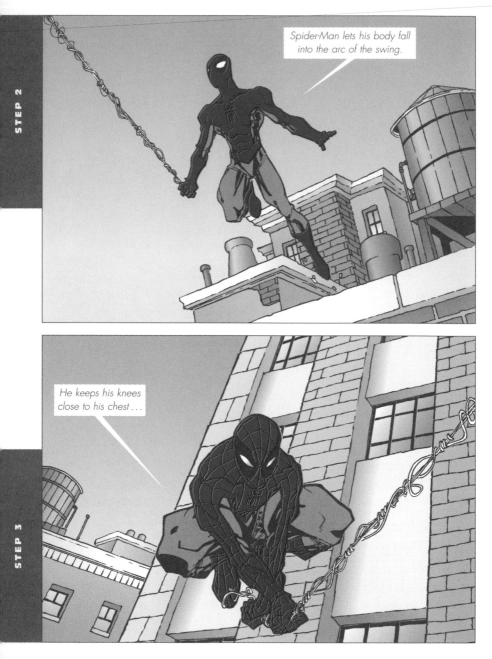

The Basics

Step 6: Switch strands when your velocity reaches zero.

As you approach the top of the arc, you'll continue to slow until finally—for one brief moment—you're just hanging there in midair. In this instant, release the first strand, tuck your knees back up to your chest, and start the process all over again.

Step 7: Come in for a smooth landing.

When you're ready to return to the ground, start by scouting out a landing zone—preferably one devoid of citizens or other obstacles (parks, low rooftops, and wide alleys work best). As you approach the ground on your final arc, think of your legs as a plane's landing gear—keep them retracted until you're just above street level. Then, at the last moment, stick out your feet and let go of the web while you're still a few inches (6–12 cm) above the runway. Remember: When you hit the ground, you'll be going upward of 30 miles per hour (48 km/h), so hit it running and stick your arms out to the sides for balance. Don't get too disheartened if your first few attempts end in bone-shattering failure. Ask any pilot, and he'll tell you that the hardest part of flying is landing. He'll also tell you that any landing you can walk away from is a good one.

And don't worry—it'll take some practice before you make building-to-building transit look as effortless as Spider-Man does. After all, in the words of Aunt May, "you're not Superman, you know."

How to Develop Your Spider-Sense

Spider-Man can lift thousands of pounds with ease, move with superhuman speed, and walk on the ceiling as easily as he walks down the street, but no power has saved his skin more often than his trusty Spider-Sense. Little is known about the mechanics of this built-in radar, which causes the base of Spidey's skull to tingle whenever danger's near. And to the Spider-Sense, "danger" covers a pretty broad spectrum. That tingling could mean a deadly hail of bullets headed his way or an axe-wielding assassin is sneaking up behind him. Or it could simply mean that the refrigerator light's about to burn out. Either way, it's an invaluable weapon in Spider-Man's crime-fighting arsenal—one that can guide him in total darkness, help him track down a hideout, and even tip him off when someone's just thinking of harming him (if only it could predict stock prices, maybe Peter could finally quit his day job). You may not get the skull-tingling hints that help Spider-Man, but you can still train your brain to think like a super hero.

Perform regular sense-strengthening exercises.
Daredevil (a once-in-a-while Spider-Man ally) found his other senses incredibly heightened after he was stricken blind by radioactive waste. Even though he'd lost his sight, his senses of taste, smell, touch, and hearing became so powerful that he "saw" the world more clearly than ever before. Granted, the radiation made those senses much stronger than nature ever could, but it demonstrates a real phenomenon: When one sense is diminished, our bodies compensate by strengthening the remaining ones. You can use this natural reaction to your advantage by artificially removing certain senses in order to heighten the others. Your senses may never be quite as sharp as Spidey's, but the following exercises can help you build up a sensory arsenal that's head and shoulders above the average human's.

- Sight: Walk around the city while wearing earplugs and take notice of how much more you scan your environment, whether crossing a busy street or standing on a subway platform.

- Hearing: Get in the habit of using idle time (sitting on a park bench, riding in an elevator) to close your eyes and listen. Try to pick out as many different sounds as you can. The hum of a street light, a lawnmower in the distance, a bird chirping . . . you'd be surprised how many sounds it takes to create what the mind perceives as silence.

- Touch: Again, close your eyes whenever you have a moment and concentrate on the world as your skin perceives it. Run your fingers over different surfaces and pay attention to their textures. Try to feel your watchband rubbing against your arm, the vibrations of a passing truck, or the subtle breeze of someone walking by.

- Smell: As you go about your day, try to count how many individual smells you can identify—the hot dog cart, the warm air from the subway vent, the perfume of a pedestrian, and the fresh-cut grass from that lawnmower you heard earlier.

HOW TO BECOME FLUENT IN BODY LANGUAGE

When you know what to look for, the body can be a window to the mind. Whether they know it or not, most humans will tell you if they're anxious, upset, uncertain, or elated—all without saying a word. And as any professional bodyguard will attest, it's the anxious ones you really have to look out for. After all, they may be anxious because they're about to take a shot at you. That's why the pros are trained to look for the following telltale physical signs of anxiety:

- **Excessive sweating:** Under the arms, on the face, or on the palms.

- **Jumpy Adam's apple:** A sign of rapid swallowing (usually associated with anxiety).

- **Folded arms:** Often misinterpreted as a sign of standoffishness, folding one's arms is actually a mechanism to provide comfort in times of stress.

- **Pursed lips/licking:** Tight or pursed lips are a sign of anxiety, and excessive licking of the lips indicates a dry mouth.

■■■■■ Take care of your body.

A super hero's body is a high-performance machine. And just like a fighter jet or a Formula 1 car, it requires regular maintenance to run at peak efficiency.

- **Get plenty of sleep:** This is a tough one for super heroes, since they typically work all day and fight crime all night. But sleep is imperative, especially for "thinking" heroes like Spider-Man. Fatigue leaves your eyes tired, your mind foggy, and your reflexes dull (a poor diet can do the same). And in this business, that can be fatal.

- **Avoid caffeine and nicotine:** First of all, if you're aspiring web-head who smokes, you need to find a new line of work. I mean, *villains* don't even smoke anymore (unless you count J. J. Jameson as a "villain," but that's up for debate). Further, caffeine and nicotine are stimulants that can leave you jittery and unable to concentrate.

- **Meditate:** Regular meditation can alleviate stress and contribute to better overall health, as well as improve your ability to stay calm and focused, even in the midst of a crisis.

■■■■■ Take stock of every environment you enter.

Whether you're swinging around the city in costume or simply walking to the corner deli in your street clothes, danger can strike at any moment. That means you need to stay alert and ready to react at all times. Maintain situational awareness by keeping track of the people (potential threats) and objects (potential hazards) in your physical space. You'll need to be constantly planning. For instance, every time you enter a building, you should note potential escape routes and take mental snapshots of the layout in case you have to find your way back in total darkness, thick smoke, or some other obstruction.

■■■■■ Look for the piece that doesn't fit.

Everyone's experienced a "gut feeling"—a moment when your subconscious sounds an alarm and warns you that something's not right. Is someone approaching too quickly? Are they wearing a heavy coat in the middle of summer, or dark glasses at night, or something else that's suspicious? Learn to listen to your gut— more often than not, it's onto something.

How to Strike Fear into Your Enemies

Some super heroes can count on sheer size to intimidate foes (the Hulk and Thing come to mind). Others have nightmarish appearances that erode the enemy's will to fight (Ghost Rider, for example). But when you're a friendly, neighborhood kind of guy—decked out in colorful tights, no less—you have to rely on more creative forms of intimidation. Spider-Man's no killer, but that's never stopped him from scaring his enemies half to death (and taking no small amount of pleasure in doing so). And he's always had a flair for drama (and for dramatic actresses). It's only fitting that some of his favorite scare tactics come straight from the world of theater.

Step 1: Turn out the lights.
Criminals like to operate at night because it offers protection from meddling cops and nosy neighbors. Spider-Man also likes to operate after hours—and not just because it's prime-crime territory. He knows that the same darkness crooks rely on can also make them tremble. Thanks to his highly tuned Spider-Sense, he can get around in the dark much better than the average knife-wielding goon. The same is true for you, assuming you've been practicing your sense-strengthening exercises (see "How to Develop Your Spider-Sense," page 39). If you're battling in an abandoned factory, stop by the fuse box before launching your attack. If you're in an alley or park, shoot thick globs of webbing over any nearby streetlights.

Step 2: Use surround sound.
As your foe begins to panic in the pitch-blackness, crank up the fear dial by surrounding him with clangs, creaks, and (if you must) clever one-liners. Do this by using a combination of speed (orbit him with your web-shooters) and deception (throw objects around to create the illusion of omnipresence). Note: If you're facing more than one opponent, skip this step and get right to the attack (see "How to Take On a Gang of Henchmen," page 89).

Step 3: Make an entrance.

Now that you've got Mr. Bad Guy quaking in his boots, send his heart rate into the stratosphere with a good old-fashioned "boo" entrance. Spidey loves to lower himself upside down on a web until he's just above the back of an unsuspecting criminal, and then . . .

Step 4: Take him up to the nosebleeds.

Snatch the startled sap off his feet and web-sling your way toward the tallest building around (the swinging sensation alone will probably leave him green with motion sickness and begging for mercy). Continue to the roof, and then hold him (preferably by the ankles) over the ledge. If it's information you need, he'll be forth-coming with it. But if he's just a simple street punk, use the opportunity to chat with him about reevaluating some of his life choices. There's something about hanging dozens of stories above the sidewalk that makes a person open to suggestions.

Step 5: Offer a coming attraction.

If Spider-Man has a particularly uncooperative criminal on his hands, he can make his point with a show of force—say, crumpling a steel bar like a piece of paper or lifting a minivan over his head. You may not have such dramatic exam-ples at your disposal, but you can still let your law-breaking friend know that you're holding all the cards. For instance, if you're on a rooftop, take one of his shoes and toss it over the edge. Let him watch its long, long, fall to the pavement below (just be careful not to smash any pedestrians' heads in).

SKIP THE SPIDER-SIGNAL

Early in his career, Spidey developed the Spider-Signal—a powerful, belt-mounted light that projected an image of his mask onto nearby surfaces. While it was certainly theatrical (remember, Peter originally hoped to milk the whole spider thing for TV stardom), it proved largely impractical in his crime-fighting role. These days, it's mostly used as an occasional distress beacon or emergency light source. Unless you're dealing with incredibly jittery thugs, announcing yourself with a slide show is more festive than frightening. At best, it causes momentary confusion. At worst, it gives away your location.

How to Maintain a Secret Identity

For someone who walks on walls, Spider-Man's a pretty regular guy. That's because unlike *some* super heroes (*cough*—billionaire playboy—*cough*), his entrée into the vigilante business wasn't the result of some dark trauma or revenge fantasy. Peter Parker was—and *is*—a wisecracker, an insatiable learner, and a well-mannered do-gooder. Spider-Man is simply an extension of those qualities—Peter Parker writ large. Make no mistake: It's Peter, not Spider-Man, who wears the mask. And wear it he must. After all, a super hero's secret identity is more than an excuse to sport an extra layer on cold days.

It's a fortress: the one place your enemies can't get to you. Where your loved ones are safe from retribution, and where *you* are safe to escape the rigors of super hero life—not to mention prosecution (see "How to Indemnify Yourself Against Legal Action," page 144). As such, it should be protected as your most cherished possession.

Trust no one.
Very few people know that Peter Parker and Spider-Man are one and the same, and with good reason. If that information ever became public, every super-villain in the Western hemisphere would make a beeline for Peter's apartment, hell-bent on exacting revenge. His friends and loved ones would be kidnapped or killed, and he'd be hounded like a celebrity (or, knowing some New Yorkers, jeered like a bum) on the street. Holding down a job would become impossible, and he would die penniless and alone in a blue and red cardboard box somewhere on Queens Boulevard.

Funny? Maybe, but the moral of the story is deadly serious: Treat your secret identity like a loaded gun—only give it to someone if you're absolutely certain she will never use it against you or allow it to fall into the wrong hands. And remember, telling someone your secret might seem like a gesture of friendly trust, but in reality, you're bestowing a heavy (and quite possibly deadly) burden on that person.

School yourself in the ordinary.
When your nights consist of foiling sinister plots and battling evil geniuses, knowing the name of a sitcom star might seem a tad trivial. However, staying current with popular culture is vital to protecting your secret identity. Draw as little attention to your civilian self as possible. Remember: You're just an ordinary lad or lass. You've heard that song everyone's singing, seen that episode everyone's talking about, and read that bestseller that they're supposedly turning into a movie. Your clothes are in style (but not flashy), you're politically informed (but not partisan), and your home is decorated in a manner consistent with your age group and income bracket.

Don't be *too* normal.
If you're a graceful, powerful super hero, it doesn't mean your daytime persona has to be clumsy and wimpy. Some crime fighters take their civilian identities too far in the other direction (*cough*—geeky newspaper reporter—*cough*), a move that can raise more suspicion than it alleviates.

On the other hand, don't be a show-off.
Sooner or later, you'll be tempted to use your spider-skills in civilian life—whether it's beating up the school bully or impressing the cute girl at the gym. Don't. Peter almost made the same mistake when he first discovered his powers. He saw an opportunity to climb the social ladder and make a few bucks in the process. But it's all fun and games until somebody loses an uncle. It's only natural to dream of fame, fortune, and glory, but being a super hero means foregoing those things in the name of the public good.

Choose a super hero–friendly career.
Unfortunately, "the public good" doesn't put food on the table. Unless you're sitting on a cave full of family money, you'll need to find a way to make a living. Peter's job as a freelance photographer is one of the best super-careers around. Not only does it afford him plenty of flexibility, it gives him an excuse to be where the action is. But working a nine-to-five office job is generally a bad idea for super heroes—your cover won't last long if you constantly have to run off for three-hour "bathroom breaks."

TEN SUPER HERO-FRIENDLY CAREERS

1. Dog walker
2. Actor
3. Interior decorator
4. Real estate agent
5. Personal trainer

6. Food critic
7. Social worker
8. Fashion model
9. Lawyer
10. College professor

Don't give away your address.
When it's time to return to that appropriately decorated home, be careful. Since webs are Spider-Man's preferred means of transportation, an enemy could theoretically track him down by following his discarded strands. Translation? Give the web-shooters a rest once you get close to home. Even better, leave a trail heading in the wrong direction and double back on foot. Make your costume change carefully, too—especially if you live in a crowded city like New York. Just because you duck into an alley doesn't mean people aren't watching from above. And changing on rooftops only works if there are no taller buildings in sight.

THE PSYCHOLOGICAL BAGGAGE OF SUPER-HERO-DOM

One of the most dangerous (and least discussed) occupational hazards for super heroes is psychological strain. Balancing the burdens of protecting an entire city with the pressures of everyday life can lead to anxiety, depression, or even total nervous collapse. When Peter took up crime fighting, he was merely a teenager (not an age noted for its psychological stability). Luckily, he was also exceptionally intelligent and had Aunt May around to give him love, support, and even-keeled wisdom. Still, the pressures of being Spider-Man have caused Peter to hang up his web-shooters "for good" more than once. As a super hero, it's imperative that you learn to compartmentalize your life. You can't let a pestering telemarketer hinder your ability to fight crime. Nor can you let a night of death and destruction ruin family brunch. Like cops and doctors, you have to leave the ugliness at the office.

Chapter 2

Spidey Skills

"Spider-Man, Spider-Man, does whatever a spider can. Spins a web, any size. Catches thieves, just like flies. Look out! Here comes the Spider-Man!"
—1960s cartoon theme song

Congratulations. You can wear a fancy outfit, climb walls, and lead a dual life. That makes you fun to have at parties—but it doesn't make you a super hero. Not yet. Stepping into Spidey's boots means facing a pungent potpourri of challenges every time you leave the house.

How to Stop a Getaway Car

You're not likely to find Spider-Man in a car* (thanks to those web-shooters, he needs a Buick like Wolverine needs a butter knife). However, you will find him *on* one from time to time—usually it's the getaway car of a desperate criminal. Should you find yourself in pursuit of maniac motorist, you'll need to act quickly and decisively. The lives of countless drivers and pedestrians are on the line—not to mention your own.

Step 1: Launch your attack from above.

There's a reason the police summon choppers to a high-speed chase. Shaking a patrol car is one thing, but shaking an aircraft? Not likely. Assuming your web-slinging skills are up to the task (see "How to Swing from Building to Building," page 34), use your shooters to zero in on the suspect vehicle from above. Match its speed. Make sure there are no obstacles coming up (traffic, pedestrians, road blocks) that would cause the driver to swerve unexpectedly (and cause you to hit pavement instead of pay dirt), and execute your landing.

Step 2: Get low and stay low.

If you land successfully, don't pat yourself on the back just yet. While Spidey's sticky appendages make it virtually impossible for him to be thrown off a car, you're considerably easier to ditch. Therefore, your first order of business should be flattening those rock-hard spider-abs against the roof. This lowers both your center of gravity and your drag coefficient. "Drag co-*what*?" you ask? It means you won't get blown off the roof by wind rushing over the car.

Step 3: Find anchor points for your hands.

If you're chasing a taxicab, this shouldn't be a problem. Same goes for cars with luggage racks or open sunroofs. But if it's a modern, smooth-topped sedan, finding something to grab on to can be a wee bit trickier. If the car is small enough, try "hugging" it by digging your fingers into the tops of the driver- and passenger-side windows. On some older cars, you might also find a gap between the windshield and the roof. If you start to lose your grip, allow yourself to slide toward

---

*Actually, Spidey did have a car for a minute or two
(see "The Spider-Mobile Fiasco," page 54).

the rear of the vehicle, and then dig your toes into the lip where the trunk meets the rear window.

Step 4: Spread your legs as far apart as possible.
Think of your feet as training wheels, bracing you against the violent swerves that the driver will undoubtedly begin once he hears the "thud" of your landing (don't be embarrassed—even Spider-Man makes a "thud" when he lands on cars).

Step 5: Anticipate gunfire.
In addition to cutting the wheel back and forth, the driver (or passengers) will almost certainly start ventilating the roof with small-arms fire. To ensure that they don't ventilate you along with it, be ready to shift your weight and roll to one side at the first hint of flying lead. Be warned, however: No matter how much rolling around you do, one of those bullets is going to find its mark sooner or later. That's why it's vital that you move to the next step as quickly as possible.

Step 6: Blind the driver with webbing.
Again, make sure that there are no innocent bystanders in the car's immediate path. Then, holding tight with one hand, aim a web-shooter at the windshield and let loose a torrent of thick webbing (one brisk trigger tap followed by a long second tap). With the glass rendered opaque, the driver will instinctively slam on the brakes. This, by the way, will send you careening through the air like a cannon ball.

Step 7: Try not to break every bone in your body.
As you rack up those frequent flyer miles (i.e., hurtle toward the asphalt), aim your web-shooters at the nearest building, fire off a strand, and swing to a graceful stop. And once you're done doing that, wake up and realize that only the *real* Spider-Man has enough speed and agility to pull it off. You're still in midair, and face it—this one's gonna hurt. But you *can* minimize the damage:

- Tuck yourself into a ball: Pull your arms and legs close to your body, and lower your head.

- Don't try to land on your feet: Unless you savor the idea of breaking both legs, ankles, and kneecaps.

- Roll when you hit the ground: This will help dissipate the energy of your impact.

THE SPIDER-MOBILE FIASCO

When Corona Motors needed a campaign to tout its new pollution-free engine, they could've settled for the obvious—a montage of pristine rivers and gleeful forest critters, perhaps. Instead, they approached our favorite web-head about building a "Spider-Mobile" (to be powered by their engine, of course). At first, Spider-Man dismissed the offer as ridiculous. You could almost hear his thoughts: "Hocking cars is for athletes and movie stars—not super heroes! Oh, the indignity! The outrage! The . . . wait, they're offering me *how* much money?" Realizing that he sorely needed the cash, Spidey came around.

When it came to building his Spider-Mobile, he enlisted the help of friend and car fanatic Johnny Storm (a.k.a. the Human Torch). Johnny cobbled together something that resembled a dune buggy wearing a leotard. Let's not mince words—this was no Batmobile, kids. Even Spidey called it a "fiasco." But looks weren't everything, and the Spider-Mobile had a few tricks up its sleeve. Standard features included web-cannons, a high-powered Spider-Signal, and an ejector seat (why Spider-Man would need an ejector seat, we may never know).

Lo and behold, Spidey drove it off a pier during his first test run (to be fair, one of his enemies, Mysterio, had altered the pier to look like a road), and it was presumed lost for good. But little did Spider-Man know that *another* enemy, Tinkerer, had salvaged the sunken Spider-Mobile and modified it to attack the super hero. Spidey eventually defeated the modified buggy and returned it (as a twisted heap of scrap) to Corona's ad agency with a "good riddance."

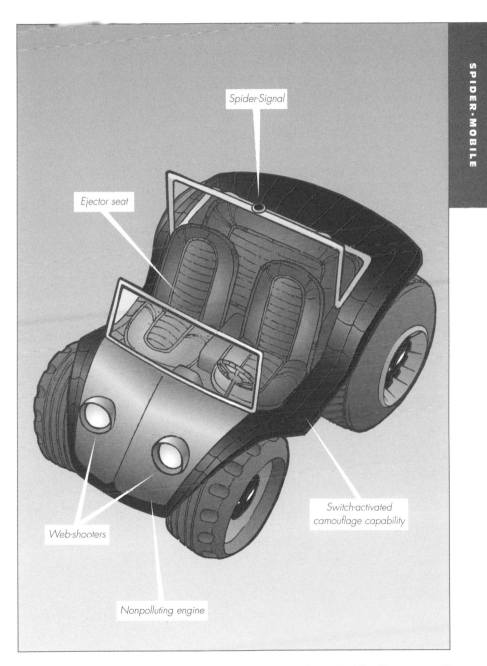

Spider-Signal

Ejector seat

Web-shooters

Nonpolluting engine

Switch-activated
camouflage capability

How to Survive a Pumpkin-Bomb Attack

One of the nastiest thorns in Spider-Man's side is that cackling, glider-wielding menace, the Green Goblin. And there's nothing that gives the Gob-father more pleasure than raining down a volley of pumpkin bombs from his turbo fan–powered perch. These "bombs," shaped like mini jack-o'-lanterns, are actually glorified grenades that can be modified to carry everything from toxic gas to good ol' explosives. Luckily, the web-slinger knows exactly what to do when the orange agents start flying.

Close the distance.
Like grenades, pumpkin bombs are usually detonated with three-, five-, or seven-second fuses. And while instinct might tell you to run for the hills, distance could actually be your enemy here. By running *toward* the Goblin, you can get a hand (or web) on those orange buggers before they've had time to arm themselves—giving you the option of hurling them back in his face or away from innocent bystanders before they blow.

Gain some altitude quickly.
Since they can carry different payloads, it's always prudent to treat a pumpkin bomb attack as a chemical or biological attack. If your Spider-Sense is well tuned, you'll see or hear the first volley coming, giving you a few precious seconds to take a deep breath, point your web-shooter toward the nearest building, and head for the penthouse. Since most chemical and biological agents are heavier than air, this move will buy you enough time to fix your sights on the nearest flag or discarded page of the *Daily Bugle* and determine the wind direction. Then, being careful to keep one eye on the Goblin's glider, get upwind as fast as your Spider-Strength will carry you before launching your counterattack.

Move the fight away from populated areas.
Even without chemicals or toxic gases, pumpkin bombs have a kill radius similar to that of a grenade: roughly 16 feet (5 m) in every direction. And as a super

hero, it's your job to make sure they're flying toward *you*, and away from any elderly hot dog vendors or groups of schoolchildren that may be nearby. Once again, altitude is your friend—and for more than one reason. First, by taking the battle above street level, you're drawing the Goblin's fire away from the good people of New York. Second, you're eliminating the enemy's vantage point (it's a whole lot harder to rain terror from below than above). But remember: Your foes are well aware of your fondness for the innocent, and what seems like a random attack could be a sinister trap.

Keep moving.

A rolling stone gathers no moss, and a moving super hero gathers no shrapnel. If you've managed to sling yourself above street level, don't be content to perch on a flagpole and admire the view. By swinging or leaping from rooftop to rooftop, you'll force the attacker to fire at a moving target from a moving platform—greatly reducing his odds of sending you to Uncle Ben before your time. However, if you find yourself grounded, you still have some escape and evasion options—try running in a random zigzag pattern to keep the attacker guessing while exhausting his supply of ammunition.

Avoid windows.

And while you run that zigzag, stay away from windows at all costs! Pumpkin bombs produce concussion waves that extend far beyond their kill radius, and these waves have a tendency to turn windows into flying shards of death. And flying shards of death have a tendency to gouge eyeballs and sever limbs.

Name: Norman Osborn II
First Appearance: *Amazing Spider-Man* #14 (1964)
Height and Weight: 5'11" (180 cm), 185 pounds (84 kg)
Powers: Superhuman strength, heightened intellect
Equipment: Goblin glider, pumpkin bombs

No villain has had a more lasting or devastating effect on Spider-Man's life. As a child, Norman Osborn's nights were tormented by dreams of a goblin-like specter, and his days troubled by the financial and professional failings of an unloving father. Norman swore he'd never make the same mistakes—he studied hard and saved money until he'd amassed enough to launch Osborn Industries with a partner, Mendel Stromm. He became a widower when the mother of his son, Harry, passed away (ironically, he'd become just as unloving as his own father). One day, Norman discovered that Stromm had been embezzling money and promptly fired him. In Stromm's notes, he discovered a formula for increasing strength and intelligence. Osborn whipped up a batch but failed to notice that a jealous Harry had switched some of the ingredients. The mixture exploded, knocking Norman unconscious.

When he awoke, he realized that he was vastly smarter and stronger (unfortunately, he missed the part about the transformation driving him completely insane). Osborn saw his new abilities as a path to even greater fortune and power—things he'd coveted since his youth. He wanted to start by uniting all of New York's most notorious criminals. And to get their attention and respect, he had the ultimate statement in mind: Kill Spider-Man.

He tried to make that statement as the Green Goblin, but Spidey managed to defeat him again and again—until the Goblin discovered the true identity of his son Harry's best friend, Peter Parker. Once he found out that Parker was Spider-Man, he kidnapped Peter's first love, Gwen Stacy (see "The Women in Spider-Man's Life," page 157), to draw him out into the open. Gwen was killed in the ensuing battle, and Spidey was so enraged that, for once, he gave serious thought to violating his "do not kill" decree. But he never got the chance. The Goblin was impaled by his glider and "died" on the spot (note the quotes). Three other men have donned the Goblin costume, including Harry.

How to Rescue Someone Who's Hanging off the Side of a Building

Civilians. It's almost like they want to make Spider-Man's life more difficult. Always getting themselves snatched up by some flying villain and tossed around like a dog's squeaky toy; always staring slack-jawed at the giant robot instead of running away; and never, ever missing an opportunity to leave their teddy bear–clutching children alone in a stampeding mob. And in a city teeming with tall buildings, you can count on at least one Jane Q. clawing the side of a skyscraper when the smoke of battle clears. For the real Spidey, this type of rescue scores a zero in degree of difficulty. He merely scurries up the side of the building and uses his superhuman strength to pull the person to safety. But for those of us with normal biochemistry, it's a smidge more complicated.

Step 1: Secure yourself.
Once you've reached the roof, ledge, or window nearest the victim, start by establishing solid footing. Look around for anything sturdy enough to support the combined weight of both bodies: a chimney or gargoyle if you're working from a roof and ledge, or a radiator or heavy piece of furniture if you're working from a window. If your web-shooters are functional, fire a strand at one of these objects, and if time permits (it usually won't), tie it around your waist. If you're out of web fluid or your web-shooters have been damaged, grab your anchor with one hand and prepare to grab the victim with the other.

Step 2: Calm the victim down.
All that flailing and hyperventilating wastes precious energy and makes your job more difficult, so it's important that you pull the victim out of the panic response. No small task, considering she's only a few fingertips away from certain death. First, assure her everything's going to be okay (especially if it isn't). Next, throw in a joke. Spider-Man is a notorious wisecracker—a talent he often uses to put others at ease. Try making light of the situation with a few clunky one-liners, like:

"I've heard of living on the edge, but this is ridiculous!" Or, "Haven't you ever heard of an elevator?"

Step 3: Dry your hands.

If you're wearing gloves, ditch 'em—they could slip off while you're trying to pull the victim to safety. Reach into your little bag of climber's chalk (see "How to Crawl up a Wall," page 17) and quickly clap some on your hands. If you're sans chalk, run those greasy palms over your costume (don't worry, it needed a trip to the dry cleaner's anyway).

Step 4: Grab the victim by the wrist.

When you extend your hand, the victim will want to grab it handshake-style. Wrong. Clasping hands puts tremendous strain on some of the body's weakest parts—namely the fingers. And unless both of you have exceptional grips, there's a good chance of those hands coming apart. Instead, grab the victim's wrist, and tell her to grab yours. This configuration creates a natural "lock" that's much more difficult to break.

 Experiment: 1) Put the book down. 2) Grab your left wrist with your right hand. 3) Grab your right wrist with your left hand. 4) Try to pull your arms apart. See? 5) Pick the book up and continue.

Step 5: Pull the victim to safety.

Ever tried to lift a full-grown person with one arm? Even with a gallon of adrenaline in your veins, it's quite the chore. Therefore, it's important that the victim uses his or her remaining strength to climb while you pull.

Spider-Man grabs the victim's wrist and instructs her to grab his.

How to Build and Fly a Web Hang Glider

All in all, it was just another day in the life of a super hero. In *Amazing Spider-Man* #157, Spidey was pursuing Doctor Octopus (see "Know Your Enemy," page 67), who was also being haunted by the ghost of a 1920s-style mobster named Hammerhead. But despite having both a spider and a specter on his tail, Doc Ock somehow managed to fall in love with Peter's Aunt May (got all that?). He snatched her up, intent on making her *Mrs.* Octopus—but Spider-Man wasn't about to forever hold his peace. He chased the would-be elopers to their helicopter and attached a web line as it took off. Shortly into the flight, Ock spotted the web-slinger dangling from the chopper and cut him loose. Free-falling a mile above ground, Spidey seemed as good as dead. But the good doctor forgot one very important detail: He's *Spider-Man*. The quick-thinking web-head spun together a hang glider and flew to safety. (We can assume that the studious Peter had read up on hang glider construction and operation at some point.) If you find yourself in need of wings, consider this your "don't crash" course.

Step 1: Build and assemble the basic hang glider components.

Hang gliders—made from lightweight fabric stretched into a delta-wing shape—are close cousins of the parachute. The pilot "hangs" beneath the wing and uses a bar to steer up, down, and side to side. Since your glider will be made entirely of web, you'll need to practice spinning and assembling different shapes and consistencies to mimic these essential parts:

- Sail: The lightweight fabric that covers the glider's delta shape—usually nylon.

- Keel, crossbar, and leading edges: The tubes (aircraft-grade aluminum) that maintain the sail's shape.

- Cables: Usually aircraft-grade steel; used to support the frame.

- Kingpost: A vertical tube that rises above the top of the sail, providing an anchor point for the steel cables.

- Control bar: A triangle of tubing that hangs beneath the keel; used by the pilot to steer the glider.

- Harness: Straps or "bags" that attach the pilot to the glider.

Step 2: Find a suitable launch site.

If you're plummeting back to earth, please feel free to skip this step. However, if you're merely taking your glider out for a practice flight, start small. Gently sloping hillsides are perfect for short runs (grass is also pretty forgiving in the event of an unscheduled nose plant). Make sure your intended flight path is clear of people and other hazards (such as power lines, roads, and tall buildings), and stay grounded if it's a windy day.

Step 3: Prepare for takeoff.

Lift the glider to your waist using the sides of the control bar, and start running down the hill as fast as your puny human legs will carry you. As the airflow over the sail approaches 20 miles per hour (32 km/h), you'll begin to feel the glider lift you into the air.

Step 4: Get airborne.

When this happens, lift your legs and allow the harness to take your full weight. In the same motion, shift your hands from the side of the control bar triangle to the base (coordinating all of this will take some practice—don't lose heart if you wind up with a mouthful of dirt).

Step 5: Steer to avoid obstacles and enemies.

Hang gliders don't have movable control surfaces (the ailerons or elevators you'd find on most powered aircraft). Instead, they rely on changes in airflow to turn. When you're hanging in the center of the glider, your weight is evenly distributed, and air flows evenly over the sail. Result? You go straight. To turn, shift your weight toward the direction you want to go (if you want to turn right, shift your weight to the right, and shift left to go left).

Step 6: Control your altitude.

Changing altitude requires changing the glider's "angle of attack" (a fancy way

Thermals and ridge lifts enable
web gliders to soar sky-high.

Leading edges

Sail

Keel

Harness

Control bar

How to Build and Fly a Web Hang Glider   65

of saying "tilting the sail forward or back"). To climb (or slow down), push the control bar forward so the nose tilts up. To descend (or speed up), pull the control bar back so the . . . you get it.

Step 7: Use thermals and ridge lifts to soar sky-high.
Experienced hang glider pilots can stay aloft for hours (the world record is 36) by using rising currents of air to regain altitude. Generally, these currents fall into one of two categories:

- Thermals: These are columns of warm air that rise up from "hot spots" on the ground (beach sand, asphalt—anything you wouldn't walk across barefoot on a hot day).

- Ridge lifts: Air that "bounces" upward off mountains and ridges.

 Since your glider's made out of webbing, and webbing is designed to dissolve after one hour, you may want to keep those flight times on the shorter side.

Step 8: Come in for a safe landing.
Locate a flat, wide open space and descend with a series of gentle dips. When you're just above the "runway," push the control bar as far away from your body as possible. This will stall the glider and allow you to make a graceful landing on your feet.

Name: Dr. Otto Octavius
First Appearance: *Amazing Spider-Man #3* (1963)
Height and Weight: 5'9" (175 cm), 245 pounds (111 kg)
Powers: Superior intellect and concentration
Equipment: Four telepathically controlled steel tentacles with pincers

Little Otto Octavius was a shy mama's boy—more interested in books than looks (a fact that didn't sit well with his blue-collar papa). He took an interest in science and worked his pudgy little tail off, eventually making a name for himself as one of the country's leading atomic researchers. But his ego seemed to grow in conjunction with his success, and may have been the driving force behind his decision to build the contraption that would alter his life forever. Otto's robotic tentacles (controlled by dials on a chest plate) were originally designed to handle dangerous atomic materials, allowing him to conduct his work with greater speed and autonomy. But all that changed when a botched experiment subjected him to a massive dose of radiation.

The accident fused the tentacles to his body, allowing him to control them telepathically. It also jarred an already fragile psyche right off the hinges. He might've been a slave to madness, but the newly christened "Doc Ock" was no slave to fashion. His outfit of choice? An orange and green ensemble complemented by thick sunglasses beneath his bowl-shaped coif. But super-villainy isn't about being stylish, it's about being sinister—and Otto had *sinister* down cold. Spider-Man used his own scientific prowess to defeat the Doc in their first meeting, and Ock's been obsessed with stomping the web slinger ever since.

Other archenemies have come and gone, but Octavius has never been far from Spidey's thoughts since their first meeting. Otto organized a group of Spider-Man's greatest enemies known as the Sinister Six to aid his quest to rid New York of the amazing arachnid. And yes, he also "fell in love" with Peter's Aunt May and led her to the altar (though there *might* have been some ulterior motives at work, seeing as May was about to inherit a nuclear reactor that would've proven very useful to the Doc).

A botched experiment fused tentacles to Doc Ock's body.

DOCTOR OCTOPUS

How to Tell the Clone from the Original

There are only three certainties in a super hero's life: death, taxes, and clones. Like old college buddies, clones just have a way of popping into your life when it's least convenient. Spider-Man's certainly dealt with his share of unauthorized copies (see "The Clone Saga," page 72), and truth be told, the web-master hasn't always had an easy time figuring out who was who. Since there isn't always time for a DNA test (clones have different mitochondria than their "originals") or fingerprinting (they have different prints, too), it pays to keep a few "clone-spotting" fundamentals in your toolbox. These tips assume the duplicates could be grown at a highly accelerated rate (something current science doesn't permit). Otherwise, the clones would never appear the same age as the original . . . and it wouldn't take a super hero to make *that* call.

▰▰▰ Look for distinguishing marks.
Sure, they might have started out with the same skin—but how they've used it could be worlds apart. Quickly scan their bodies for anything that suggests a more "fully lived" life—scars, piercing holes, sun damage, and, of course, ink (a lab-grown clone is less likely to have gotten that regrettable tattoo on spring break). As an adventurous archaeologist once said, "It's not the years, honey . . . it's the mileage."

THE BELLY-BUTTON FALLACY

It doesn't matter if they're hatched in the laboratories of evil geniuses or grown the old-fashioned way (in human hosts); all clones have belly buttons, despite popular opinion to the contrary. Whether it's a petri dish or a womb, embryos need oxygen and nutrients to survive, and human embryos get theirs though umbilical cords. If your clone is missing a belly button, it's actually an evil robot, not an evil clone (don't kick yourself—it's a common rookie mistake).

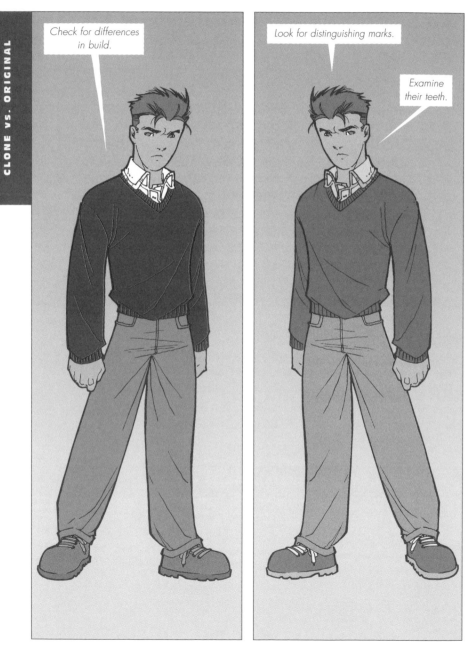

Examine their teeth.

A little amateur dentistry can help determine who's who. If one person's teeth are straight and the other's are crooked, chances are Mr. Crooked is your clone. Both people would've started with the same set of teeth, but if one's are straighter, it's likely that braces were involved. And generally speaking, accelerated-growth clones don't have too much time for their awkward phases.

Check for differences in build.

Unless the clone-maker has taken his subject's diet and exercise habits into consideration, it's unlikely that the copy and the original would have exactly the same build. This is helpful if you know something about the original person's lifestyle (if you know that the *real* John Smith is a fitness instructor, a potbelly would probably raise suspicion). Even if you don't, a well-toned body is often indicative of a real person, since going to the gym isn't something most clones would have the time or inclination to do.

Examine their general health and appearance.

Experiments in animal cloning suggest that the copies are more prone to disease than the originals. There's also evidence that clones age faster than the rest of us. Therefore, if one of your subjects seems sickly, you may have your culprit.

Give them a history quiz.

A body can be copied right down to the last nose hair, but it's a little trickier to clone someone's memories. Even a clone who studied the original's life couldn't possibly know every little detail, especially when it came to "off the record" information like first kisses and embarrassing nicknames. Grill both subjects on the things that only the real one could know (obviously, this only works if you have the right information to compare their answers to, or if you share some personal history with the original).

Note changes in behavior.

Some personality traits come preloaded, but most are products of the environment. If a normally aggressive person is suddenly passive, something's wrong. Remember: They might look identical, but their pasts couldn't be more different.

██████ And if all else fails . . .

Whoever points his finger at the other and says, "He's the clone, shoot him!" is always the clone.

THE CLONE SAGA

Spidey's "clone saga" began when an enemy (the Jackal) somehow created a perfect copy of Peter Parker, complete with all of his powers and memories. After being captured, Spider-Man awoke to find himself face to face with . . . Spider-Man. The two web-slingers rumbled at first but quickly teamed up to save the clone of Peter's first love, Gwen Stacy (see "The Women in Spider-Man's Life," page 157). The new Spidey took the name Ben Reilly—Ben after his beloved uncle, and Reilly from his Aunt May's maiden name. Neither Peter nor Ben was sure which one of them was the original and which was the clone, a problem that eventually drove Peter to the brink of madness (especially after tests indicated that *he* was the copy). This uncertainty lingered for years (the clone saga spanned more than one hundred issues) until Spider-Ben finally sacrificed his life to save Spider-Pete. As he died in Peter's arms, Ben's body turned to dust—proving once and for all that Parker, not Reilly, had been the real deal all along.

How to Rescue Children from a School Bus That's Teetering over the Edge

It's every crime fighter's nightmare: A bus full of panicked children hangs perilously over the edge of a cliff or bridge, the driver unconscious or dead. You can hear the moans of the overstressed frame buckling—the desperate cries of the passengers as they press their faces against the glass. Waiting around for the fire department isn't an option. This baby's gonna go, and you'd better move fast. Spider-Man's tasted just about every flavor of the "kids in danger" scenario, and thankfully he's yet to lose a single nose-picker. But snatching children from the jaws of death isn't as easy as Spidey makes it look.

Step 1: Anchor the bus if possible.
If the bus is hanging from a bridge or overpass, shoot a few thick web strands onto the undercarriage (the strongest part of the bus) and tie them around the nearest steel beam or concrete block. If there's nothing to anchor to (or if you've left home without your shooters—shame on you), commandeer the nearest car and park it right up against the rear bumper. Then, use anything you can get your hands on—jumper cables, bungee cords, rope—to tie the bus and car together.

Step 2: Check your ego at the door.
Don't hesitate to ask for help from bystanders. Use them to tie off anchors, stop traffic, or even hang onto the back of the bus if necessary. You need every available advantage when lives are on the line (especially young lives), so save the loner super hero bit for another day.

Step 3: Calm the passengers.
Easier said than done. Most adults—let alone grade-school kids—have a tough time keeping it together when they're staring death in the eye. But for obvious reasons, it's crucial that you keep them as still as possible. Start by reassuring them that help is here, and that they're going to be okay. Young kids feel more

comfortable with structure, so try turning the rescue into a game of Simon Says. Tell them to pay very close attention to your instructions and not to do anything unless it's preceded by those magic words.

Step 4:   Assess the danger of an imminent fall.
The rule of thumb is, the higher the rear wheels are off the ground, the less time you have. A school bus's tipping point is *not* in the middle. In fact, it's closer to the front or rear axle. If you're lucky, the bus in question is a rear-engine model (your first clue would be the absence of a rear emergency door) and the center of gravity is working in your favor. But if it's a "traditional" school bus, its engine (all 1,500–1,800 pounds [680–815 kg] of it) is hanging perilously over the edge. Keep in mind that most buses have rear- or center-mounted fuel tanks with a maximum capacity of 70 gallons (265 l). That means even a freshly filled tank will only provide about 500 pounds (227 kg) of counterbalance.

Step 5:   Instruct the passengers to move toward the rear of the bus.
Simon says hold hands as tightly as you can and walk *slowly* toward the rear in single file.

Step 6:   Slowly open the rear emergency door.
Whether it's in the back or on the side of the bus, the emergency exit will have a lever that allows you to open it from the outside. Since the tail of the bus is probably several feet off the asphalt, you might need to stand on top of another vehicle (or sit on a bystander's shoulders) to reach it.

Step 7:   Tell the children to keep holding hands as they exit.
Grab the kids one by one and hand them off to your helpers (if you're alone, just toss them to safety). For those kids still inside the bus, keep reminding them to hold hands as tightly as possible until they reach the exit. In the event that the bus slides over the edge while they're still inside, the kids may be able to hold on to each other as it falls away.

Spider-Man uses web strands to anchor the bus.

He carefully opens the rear door . . .

. . . and instructs the children to hold hands tightly while exiting the bus.

How to Rescue Children from a School Bus   75

SPIDER-PALS

Even a super hero of Spider-Man's caliber can't always go it alone. When he needs help, the webbed one frequently turns to his fellow super–New Yorkers.

The Fantastic Four

They were the world's first "super-team"—a group of friends (and relatives) who gained their powers from accidental exposure to cosmic radiation. Led by wealthy scientist Reed Richards (Mr. Fantastic), the foursome includes his wife, Sue (the Invisible Woman); her brother, Johnny Storm (the Human Torch); and their friend, Ben Grimm (Thing). Spider-Man counts them among his closest allies—especially Johnny, who he's teamed with dozens of times.
Mailing Address: The Baxter Building, Four Freedoms Plaza, New York, NY

The Avengers

They're the veritable "All-Star Team" of super heroes—a group of powerful allies who band together whenever a foe is too dangerous to face alone. Unlike other super-groups, the Avengers' roster is ever-changing (members have included Captain America, the Incredible Hulk, Thor, Iron Man, and just about every hero in the Marvel Universe). They're housed and financed by Iron Man's alter ego, the megawealthy Tony Stark. Stark's butler, Edwin Jarvis, is a confidant and advisor to the group.
Mailing Address: Stark Tower, 890 Fifth Avenue, New York, NY

X-Men

Charles Xavier (Professor X) uses his family fortune and mansion to run the Xavier Institute for Higher Learning, a haven for young mutants in the guise of a boarding school for "gifted youngsters." The mansion also serves as the base of operations for Xavier's handpicked band of mutant mercenaries, the X-Men, sworn to protect humanity from mutants who'd rather eradicate "normal" people than coexist with them. Its members include Wolverine, Rouge, Cyclops, Storm, and Iceman.
Mailing Address: Xavier Institute for Higher Learning, 1407 Graymalkin Lane, Salem Center, NY

How to Defeat a Shape-Shifting Opponent

Battling a super-foe is hard enough, but when that foe has the ability to alter the shape and consistency of her body? Then it's just downright annoying. Spider-Man has faced off with his share of shape-shifters, from Hydro-Man—who could turn any part of his body into a jet of water—to the Swarm—who was made entirely of bees (see "Spider-Man's Weirdest Foes," page 104). But his most frequent multimorphing opponent is the Sandman (see "Know Your Enemy," page 80), a human beach who can attack with rock-hard hammer fists one second and disappear in a cloud of dust the next. With such a wide array of attack options on the table, fighting a shape-shifter requires a super hero's mind to be as flexible as his opponent's body.

Avoid close-quarters combat.
Strong as you may be, this is no time for going toe-to-toe. Getting too close only gives your adversary more chances to use her saber-arms to slice you in half, or frying-pan fists to bash in your face. Besides, punches and kicks aren't likely to do much good. They'd either pass right through the shifter's body or bounce off and leave you with broken knuckles. Keep your distance while you formulate a plan.

Determine the composition of the shifter's body.
Spider-Man knows that Hydro-Man is made of water and that the Sandman is made of, well . . . *sand*. And that knowledge affects his fighting strategy. For instance, Spidey once defeated Hydro-Man by tricking the watery rapscallion into chasing him over a series of hot rooftops, causing the villain to slowly evaporate away. The composition of your enemy will dictate the method of her destruction. Is she made of liquid metal? Granny Smith apples? Cotton balls soaked in gasoline? (If the latter, you might consider simply tossing a lit match at her).

Use the thermostat as a weapon.
If there's one thing shape-shifters can't stand, it's extreme temperatures. Therefore, it behooves you to lure the enemy into places where very hot or very cold things

are kept, such as steel mills and cryogenics labs (one of these always seems to be nearby whenever super-beings do battle).

◼◼◼◼ Use a taser gun.

If Spidey ever got Electro (see "Know Your Enemy," page 119) on his side, he could zap the Sandman with enough amps to turn him into "Glassman" (talk about your shattering defeats). No matter what your opponent is made of, a healthy dose of electricity can interrupt shape-shifting abilities—just as it interferes with muscle control in nonmorphing folks—and give you time to trap the shifter. You can achieve this shock with a taser gun, a nonlethal weapon that fires a pair of barbs into a suspect's skin. Wires connect these barbs to the gun, which delivers a 50,000-volt charge and takes the fight right out of most people. As long as both barbs make contact with some part of the shifter (inside or out), she's in for a shock.

◼◼◼◼ If all else fails, use the nearest industrial strength vacuum.

During his first meeting with the Sandman, Spidey used a decidedly nonsuper weapon to secure victory: a vacuum cleaner. He waited until ol' Sandy was in midmorph and then sucked him to justice. It just goes to show you that being a super hero isn't always glamorous and requires your thinking to be as quick as your reflexes.

During his first encounter with the Sandman, Spider-Man used a vacuum cleaner to defeat the shape-shifting villain.

Name: William Baker (a.k.a. Flint Marko)
First Appearance: *Amazing Spider-Man* #4 (1963)
Height and Weight: 6'1" (185 cm), 240–450 pounds (109–204 kg)
Powers: Ability to transform his body into a sandlike substance, ability to alter his size and weight by incorporating nearby sand

Cue the violins. William Baker was raised by his impoverished mother in a rough-and-tumble section of Queens. He grew up on the streets, learning to cheat, steal, and bully (easy for a kid his size) at a young age. By his teens, he was a promising football player—maybe even good enough for the pros. But all that ended when he was caught throwing an important game for money. Baker was kicked off the squad and expelled from school, leaving him more aimless and bitter than ever.

William went back to the streets, taking work as a mob enforcer. He adopted the name Flint Marko because he didn't want his mother to find out about his new career. While working in the underworld, he fell in love with a pretty young thing named Marcy Conroy. But before he could put a ring on her finger, Marko was sent to the slammer. A few years in solitary confinement didn't exactly improve his disposition, and to make matters worse, he found out that Marcy had cheated on him with another hood named Vic Collins. After his release, Marko "took care" of Collins, was jailed again, escaped, and headed out on a one-man crime spree with the FBI hot on his tail.

Marko's spree took him to Savannah, Georgia, where he decided to catch a few winks on a beach. But while he napped, a nearby nuclear reactor malfunctioned, blasting him with a massive dose of radiation. When Marko came to, he discovered that he could transform any part of his body into a sandlike substance—he could become hard as stone, slip beneath a door, and increase his mass by mixing with other sand. Armed with these new powers, he officially entered the realm of super-criminal as "the Sandman" and came to Spider-Man's attention. But although he possessed incredible strength and versatility, the Sandman's limited intellect allowed the vastly smarter Spidey to outwit him again and again.

How to Survive Falling from a Tall Building

When skyscraper rooftops are your place of business, you're bound to experience an unintentional free fall sooner or later. For the Arachknight, plummeting from tall buildings toward inevitable death is about as problematic as, say, running low on cell phone minutes. That's because he's got some pretty impressive safety features: the web-shooting skills to spin a makeshift bungee cord, parachute, or fully-functional aircraft in midair (see "How to Build and Fly a Web Hang Glider," page 63); the superhuman reflexes to act quickly; and the incredible strength to survive impacts that would shatter the bodies of ordinary people. But for you Spider-Men (and -Women) in training, performing a double gainer off the Empire State Building would leave a much more significant impression on your day (not to mention 34th Street). That is, unless you have the presence of mind to follow these super-heroic steps . . .

Step 1: Shoot first, ask questions later.
You're locked in hand-to-hand combat atop the Chrysler Building's famous spire when your opponent lands a devastating roundhouse to your midsection. You tumble noisily (and painfully) down the tiered embankment until suddenly everything goes quiet. You're free-falling 1,000 feet (305 m) above Lexington Avenue, and assuming you're in the 170-pound (77 kg) range, you'll reach it in roughly eight seconds. If you've perfected those web-shooters, then there's no time like the present: Fire both barrels at everything in sight. Yes, you'll probably smack into the side of the building and crack a few ribs—but consider the alternative. However, if you're still trying to perfect that shear-thinning adhesive fluid, or if your shooters malfunction (all things mechanical are subject to failure), then you'd better implement plan B in a hurry.

Step 2: Slow your rate of descent.
The good news? One thousand feet (305 m) isn't enough room for a 170-pound (77 kg) object to reach terminal velocity. The bad news? That means you'll

continue to accelerate all the way down. Unless, of course, you find a way to counter some of that deadly gravitational force. As you fall, keep your belly pointed at the ground and look for anything that might help slow your fall: flag-poles, fabric awnings, exterior lights, gargoyles, fire escapes, terraces, or nearby rooftops. Many buildings (especially older ones) get gradually wider as they get closer to the ground. Landing on a terrace after a 50-foot (15 m) plunge is no picnic, but it's a lot better than landing on a hot dog cart after 1,000 feet (305 m).

NEW YORK CITY'S TEN TALLEST BUILDINGS

1. **The Freedom Tower** (Planned completion 2010): 1,776 feet (541 m)
2. **The Empire State Building** (1931): 1,250 feet (381 m)
3. **The Chrysler Building** (1930): 1,048 feet (319 m)
4. **American International Building** (1932): 952 feet (290 m)
5. **The Trump Building** (1930): 927 feet (283 m)
6. **Citigroup Center** (1977): 915 feet (279 m)
7. **Trump World Tower** (2001): 860 feet (262 m)
8. **Bloomberg Tower** (2005): 856 feet (261 m)
9. **The GE Building** (1933): 850 feet (259 m)
10. **CitySpire Center** (1987): 814 feet (248 m)

Step 3: Scan the ground for preferable landing spots.

Okay, so finding ways to slow your fall didn't quite work out, and now you can almost read the ads on the taxis below. But don't count yourself out just yet. Are there surfaces that might be more forgiving than concrete and asphalt? Leafy trees? Dumpsters? Snow drifts? Bodies of water? Flatbed trucks carrying pillows and mattresses?

Step 4: Twist your body to land on your back.

It should be noted that if you're falling onto a hard surface from a height of 60 feet (18 m) or more and you haven't managed to slow you rate of descent, then it doesn't really matter what part of your body hits the ground first. In the words of one panicky space marine, "Game over, man." However, for shorter, slower falls, landing on your back can minimize injury. Instinct will make you eager to land on your feet. Not a good idea. They'll break like Grandma's china. Instead, try to keep your legs horizontal and turn your body so your shoulders and upper back are the first to hit.

Step 5: Dissipate the energy of your impact.
If you can't land on your back, distribute the energy you've built while falling. Judo masters "break" falls by smacking the ground with their palms at the moment of impact, thus transferring some of the energy away from their bones and vital organs. Granted, they're usually falling from a standing height (and onto a gym mat, no less), but like they say: Every little bit helps.

AND THE WORLD RECORD FOR FALLING GOES TO . . .

On January 26, 1972, Vesna Vulović set a world record by falling 33,000 feet (10,058 m) without a parachute . . . and living to tell about it. Vulović was a 22-year-old flight attendant for Yugoslavian carrier JAT. On the day in question, she was assigned to flight 364—a flight that was suddenly and violently ripped apart by a terrorist's bomb in midair. Vesna had been strapped in her flight attendant's seat at the moment of detonation, and she remained attached—unconscious—to a large chunk of aircraft debris as it fell more than six miles (10 km) to the snow-covered mountains below. The thick snow and angled mountaintop cushioned her landing; although she suffered critical injuries and temporary paralysis, she survived (and eventually returned to work for the airline).

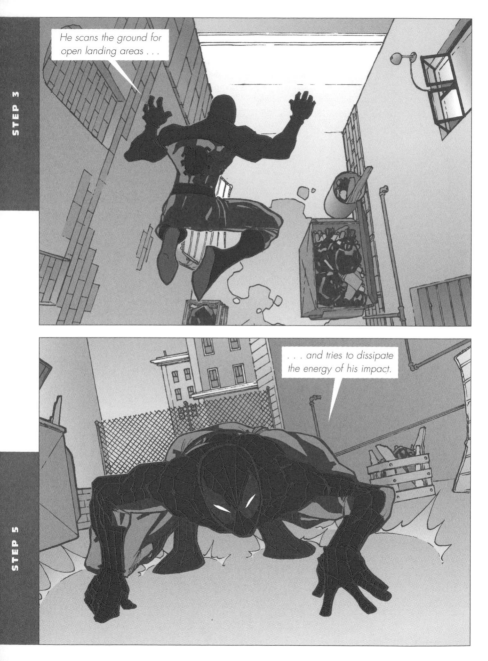

Spidey Skills

Chapter 3

Fight and Flight Skills

"Do not hit at all if it can be avoided, but never hit softly."
—Theodore Roosevelt

Spider-Man's not a violent guy. That said, he never fails to deliver a world-class beating when left with no alternative, or to escape when the odds are stacked against him. And he never, *ever* hits softly . . .

How to Take On a Gang of Henchmen

It never fails. Using a trusty spider-tracer (see "How to Make and Plant a Tracking Device," page 137), you track down the enemy's secret lair only to find it protected by a gaggle of goons. Goons with guns, no less. Super hero or not, facing multiple opponents is nothing to take lightly. In the movies, Spider-Man's enemies politely wait for their well-choreographed attack cues. But this is no movie—and when the fists (and bullets) start flying, these fundamentals could mean the difference between life and death.

Take the bad guys by surprise.

When you're outnumbered, you need every advantage you can get— and there's no greater advantage than the element of surprise. Sure, it's tempting to taunt foes by slinging clever one-liners from a darkened vantage point, or strike fear by starting the conveyor belt in their factory hideout. Dramatic? Yes, but foolish. Giving your enemies even one second of extra reaction time is giving them too much.

Use your senses.

When you launch your attack, strike fast, strike hard, and stay aware. While fighting the opponent in front of you, pay attention to your peripheral vision, and keep your ears on the footsteps (or gun clicks) of the henchmen behind you. A well-tuned nose comes in handy, too—especially if your enemies have worked up a sweat or armed themselves with odiferous weapons like flamethrowers. As you fight, keep track of your surroundings. Where are the nearest exits? How close are you to that cauldron of radioactive lava? You may not have Spider-Man's coveted Spider-Sense, but the combination of well-trained eyes, ears, nose, skin, and taste buds is a pretty good substitute (see "How to Develop Your Spider-Sense," page 39).

Make an example of the big guy.

A little psychology can be just as effective as a flying kick to the head. Once the fight begins, your first order of business should be finding the biggest, toughest henchman in the room and laying some serious hurt on him. Start by socking his nose with a quick jab. His eyes will instantly water, putting him at a tactical disadvantage. Even better, blood will run out of his nostrils (don't worry, he'll be fine), giving his companions a frightening glimpse into their immediate futures. Next, a powerful kick to the groin will send him to the floor and shatter his will to fight. When the other goons see what's happened to their prizefighter, they'll be less motivated to take you on.

Leave your scruples at the door.
Spider-Man doesn't fight dirty, but if you want to get yourself out of this situation, you can't be Mr. Nice Guy. When facing multiple attackers, a hero's goal shifts from winning to surviving—so there's nothing wrong with using your fingernails, pulling hair, or even biting if necessary.

Plan an escape route, and use it as soon as possible.
The longer this fight lasts, the more the odds shift in your opponents' favor. And since you're no good to anybody in a casket, it's your duty to get out while you can. Once you've thinned out the bad guys' ranks a little, use your web-shooter to temporarily immobilize the remaining goons while you swing your way to safety.

KNOW YOUR POLICE CODES

These codes are used by various North American law enforcement agencies.

187: murder
207: kidnapping
211: robbery
215: carjacking

999: officer needs assistance
998: officer involved in shooting
962: suspect armed and dangerous
10-13: emergency backup needed
11-41: ambulance needed

Code 3: respond quickly with lights and siren

TA: traffic accident
ADW: assault with a deadly weapon

Spider-Man lurks above his opponents,
preparing to take them by surprise.

How to Take On a Gang of Henchmen   91

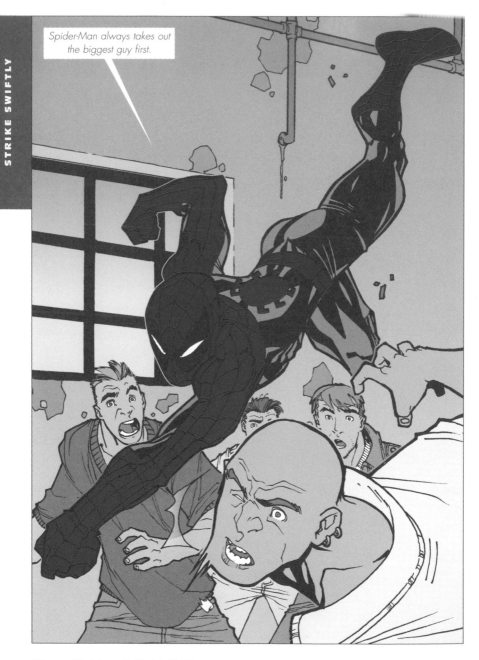

Spider-Man always takes out the biggest guy first.

How to Escape When You're a Prisoner in the Enemy's Secret Headquarters

You awake in a stark, windowless room buzzing with the sounds of high-tech computer equipment and fluorescent lights. After a few foggy moments, your eyes focus on the familiar shape of your archnemesis hovering over your chair. Instinctively you try to strike, but your hands have been cuffed (he cackles at your futile efforts to break free). It would seem all is lost.

But shame on you for being so negative. Right now, priority one is getting you out of here in one piece. The real Spider-Man would simply break his bindings like tissue paper and fight his way out the front door. But that's not an option. Your web-shooters have almost certainly been confiscated. And who knows how many of those henchman stand between you and freedom? Your best bet is living to fight another day. Of course, that means you'll have to *live* . . .

Step 1: Wait until the villain leaves you with a single incompetent guard to make your move.

Don't worry, he will. If archvillains have an Achilles' heel, it's their flair for drama. Rather than killing you outright, your nemesis won't be able to resist divulging the details of his sinister plot. He'll also taunt you for being helpless to stop it, and throw in some personal zingers like "I'll be sure to pay that pretty girlfriend of yours a visit." Then, inexplicably, he and his cadre of goons will leave the room—presumably to grab some coffee in the evil company kitchenette and dissect the previous evening's *Gilmore Girls*. In doing so, he'll leave you with the dimmest guard on the payroll.

Step 2: Draw the guard close.

You have a few options here, some better than others. Feigning a medical emergency is quick and easy, but risky (the guard might be frightened into running for help). Taking a psychological approach is a better idea. If the guard is a "tough guy" type, try taunting him with challenges to his masculinity. But if he's more of a whipping boy, you might have luck with the "why do you take his abuse?" routine.

Step 3: Sweep the legs and knock him out.
Once you've drawn the guard into your sphere of physical influence, sweep his legs out from under him and render him unconscious with a swift, well-placed kick to the noggin.

Step 4: Get your hands in front of you.
You will probably be handcuffed with your hands behind your back. Sit on the floor and slide your arms under your legs.

Step 5: Unlock your handcuffs with your key.
You *do* carry a handcuff key at all times, right? A standard series handcuff key only costs a few dollars and should be hidden in the lining of your shoes at all times. Nine times out of ten, of course, the unconscious guard will also carry a key—but you never know when your luck will run out.

Step 6: Steal the guard's uniform.
Ditch your Spider-Suit and slip into his henchman outfit. Next, drag his unconscious, underwear-clad body behind the plutonium tanks or ammo crates that are bound to be close by.

Step 7: Open the grate of the nearest ventilation shaft.
Since most secret headquarters are 1) deep beneath Earth's surface, 2) in space, or 3) in a volcano, there will almost certainly be at least one air duct in the room. Quickly rip its cover from the wall and leave it on the floor where it can't be missed.

Step 8: Trigger the alarm.
Generally, this will be indicated by a big red button or lever marked "alarm."

Step 9: Lie face down.

When the alarm sounds, the villain and his henchmen will come running. When they burst into the room, they'll see the unconscious guard (you in disguise) and busted ventilation cover and assume you're in the air ducts. The archvillain will order his goons to fan out and hunt you down.

Step 10: When the villain and his henchmen disperse, slip into the corridor. The alarms are going off, and the headquarters are suddenly overflowing with henchmen. No one will notice the uniformed lackey casually heading for the exit.

Spider-Man sweeps the guard's legs.

STEP 3

He opens the ventilation shaft . . .

. . . and triggers the alarm.

Fight and Flight Skills

When goons rush into the room, Spider-Man sneaks out behind them.

COMMON SUPER-VILLAIN HEADQUARTERS HAZARDS

As you make your way to freedom, be on the lookout for these dangerous secret-hideout staples:

- The lava pit teeming with venomous robot babies.

- The broom closet of doom.

- The scholarly yet insane orangutan that's been chained up for decades.

- The stairway to another dimension.

- The ridiculously overpriced gift shop.

GIFT SHOP

Overpriced gift shop

Broom closet of doom

Insane orangutan

Lava pit teeming with venomous robot babies

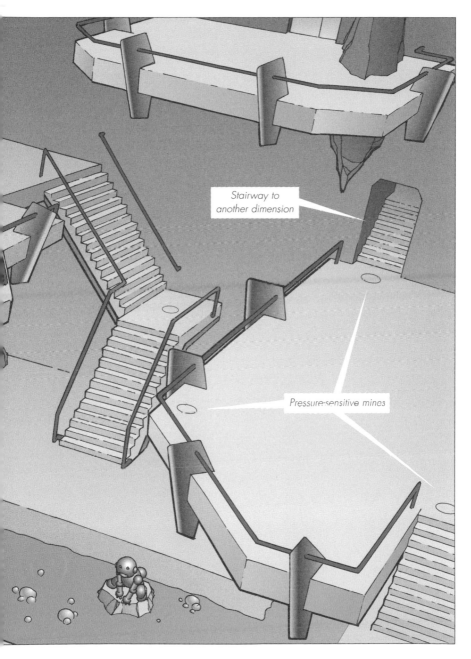

How to Disarm a Gun-Wielding Punk

Spider-Man wouldn't be caught dead with a gun in his hand. Guns are beneath the dignity of a skilled superhuman, and besides: Spider-Man's no killer. But as a crime fighter, it's only a matter of time before you (like Spidey) find yourself on the business end of some lowlife's piece. And while it's usually a good idea to avoid fighting those pistol-packing punks (pride heals quicker than flesh), sometimes the situation calls for immediate action. If you're in imminent danger of getting perforated, this quick series of moves can turn the tables. (Note: These instructions assume the gun is in your opponent's right hand. If not, hold this book up to a mirror and proceed).

Step 1: Quickly step to the left and pivot counterclockwise.
Assuming you're standing face-to-face with the attacker, step diagonally to your left and spin counterclockwise. Your shoulders should now be at a 90-degree angle to the punk's, with your back to his face.

Step 2: Grab the punk's right wrist with your right hand.
With your palm facing the ground, grab as close to the gun handle as possible—where the wrist and hand meet—and squeeze with all your might. Be fast: Your opponent will instinctively start pulling his arm back when you start to move.

According to a *New England Journal of Medicine* study, guns are 43 times more likely to kill their owners, a friend, or a relative than an attacker. And according to the Centers for Disease Control, there are about 15,000 accidental shootings in the United States each year.

Step 3: Grab the barrel with your left hand.
With your palm facing up, grab the gun's barrel from the bottom with your left hand. And for reasons too obvious to mention, make sure that no part of your hand protrudes over the end of the barrel.

Step 4: Push down with your right hand; pull up with your left.
You're trying to accomplish two things here. First, you want to aim the barrel toward the heavens. Second, you're putting pressure on the attacker's trigger finger by bending it backward.

Step 5: Yank the gun out of the punk's hand.
Hopefully you'll have heard the snap of the attacker's right index finger breaking, accompanied by an ear-shattering yelp of pain. With the barrel remaining straight up, yank the gun away by pulling down hard with your left hand.

Step 6: Remove the gun from the equation.
A lesser crime fighter might be tempted to turn the gun on the attacker. But not only is that a classless move (you're a friendly web-slinger, not a trigger-happy vigilante), it's also a stupid one. By holding on to the gun, you're only inviting the enemy to take it right back (and next time, he won't hesitate to shoot). Once you have the gun in your grasp, throw it as far away as possible, and proceed to whup your enemy the old-fashioned way.

Fight and Flight Skills

SPIDER-MAN'S WEIRDEST FOES

Spidey's squared off against all sorts of foes over the years, from a jet-powered skateboarder to a woman who thought she was the white rabbit from *Alice in Wonderland*. With that kind of competition, you have to be something truly spectacular to earn a "weird" badge. Here are a few villains who make the grade:

- **The Living Brain:** Before there was a Terminator, there was . . . the Living Brain! This evil robot had the ability to analyze and overcome every situation—including countering anything an attacker might throw its way. Unfortunately, it was the 1960s, and unlike the sleek robot villains to come, the Brain resembled an entertainment center with stubby legs.

- **Baron Ludwig von Schtupf:** The Baron (who also called himself the "Monster Maker" to further confuse the post office) was your typical castle-dwelling mad scientist with his own teleportation machine and standard-issue "take over the world" complex. He captured Spider-Man and—this is no joke—the Frankenstein monster in order to study them and make an army of Franken-Spider hybrids. Needless to say, it never quite worked out.

- **Kangaroo:** There were actually *two* Kangaroos. The first was a superior (though not superhuman) athlete who used his impressive jumping abilities for evil. He also used jet boots to enhance his leaping, and when he died, an admirer carried the torch. The second Kangaroo enhanced his jumps with an exoskeletal suit—complete with prehensile tail, pouch, and all.

- **Big Wheel:** Jackson Wheel (recipient of the World's Most Foreshadowing Name Award) enlisted the aid of the Tinkerer to build a mechanized vehicle that would further his criminal ambitions. The result? A one-wheeled disk of death, complete with machine guns, cannons, and robotic grippers. It could even scale walls! What it couldn't do? Be cool.

- **The Painter:** The Painter? Weird? Hardly. He was just another mysterious artist whose skin was partially made of canvas, and who was always covered in cockroaches for reasons unknown. An artist with the power to conjure real objects simply by painting them with his ever-present brushes.

- **The Spot:** The Spot's costume was covered in, well, spots. But not just any old spots. These spots were actually portals to another dimension (the "Spot Dimension"). They could be peeled off and stuck to different surfaces and also proved handy in combat. If you punched one of the spots, your hand would simply reemerge from another of his spots (you might even end up punching yourself).

- **The Hypno-Hustler:** Wearing his funktastic outfit of white spandex, moon boots, and spinning spiral sunglasses, the Hypno-Hustler was a seventies-era musician with a penchant for petty theft. Backed up by his band, the Mercy Killers, he would hypnotize his audiences and then proceed to rob them blind. Too bad he didn't make it to the digital age, or he could've uttered terrible catch phrases like "You pirated music, now music's pirating you!"

- **Stilt-Man:** Poor, poor Stilt-Man. He's the Rodney Dangerfield of super-villains. Try as he might, no one really considers him much of a threat. Maybe it's because his only powers come from a suit with legs that extend to over 250 feet (76 m). A suit that needs to be recharged every 24 hours. And while that might make him a superb window washer or traffic reporter, it's not quite A-list bad guy material.

- **The Swarm:** Fritz von Meyer was an ex-Nazi who fled to South America. While in hiding, he happened upon a hive of bees that had been mutated by a meteorite, and through a scientific mishap, he became the Swarm—a man made entirely of bees (great—all we need is a *flying* Nazi). He's impervious to punches and bullets and can form any number of shapes. However, Spidey's been known to defeat him with bug spray.

- **Chtylok, the Che-k'n Kau:** Unquestionably the weirdest foe Spider-Man has ever encountered. Chtylok was a giant birdlike creature worshipped by the ancient Fall People of the Savage Land (think "Antarctica"). He slumbered for 1,000 years, until ozone depletion caused his glacier-tomb to melt. The feathered fiend was plenty ticked when he woke up, especially after encountering Spider-Man and friends. The fact that Spidey called him "the Chicken Cow" and "Foghorn" probably didn't help, either.

How to Withstand a Savage Beating

Spider-Man knows how to take his lumps. He's been crushed beneath tons of steel, plummeted off the Brooklyn Bridge, and taken more right hooks than a prizefighter. It's all in a day's work for the web-slinger, who has the not-so-tiny advantage of superhuman strength on his side—strength that allows him to survive punishment a normal human couldn't. A normal human like *you*, for instance. Strong as you may be, there are limits to what the body can take. When you find yourself locked in the throes of hand-to-hand combat, knowing some simple defensive techniques can keep you on your feet and keep all your little bones and organs right where they're supposed to be. Remember, savage beatings are like gifts: It's better to give than receive.

Body Blows

▓▓▓◯❂◯ Tighten your abdominals.
Your heart and lungs have a rib cage protecting them, but the tender morsels in your belly (especially the stomach, spleen, intestines, and liver) are out in the open. Believe it or not, a single gut punch can knock you out cold—or even kill you. Keep those abs clenched.

▓▓▓◯❂◯ Turn to the side so the punches hit off center.
If you watch two trained fighters go head-to-head, you'll notice they stand at angles to one another. It's no accident. Fighting with your profile has several advantages:

- It makes you a smaller target.

- It extends your reach.

- It allows you to brace on your back foot, aiding your balance and lending more power to your strikes.

- It protects your vital organs from direct hits.

If you have to take a body blow, it's best to absorb it with your oblique muscles (beneath your love handles). Sure, there's a bigger risk of cracking a rib, but that's a small price to pay for protecting your internal organs.

 Control your breathing.

Amateur combatants have a tendency to hold their breath during a fight (no big deal, since most street brawls are over in a matter of seconds). But poor breathing techniques have no place in the crime fighter's repertoire. They'll rob you of energy, and worse, put you at risk for getting the wind knocked out of you (taking a hit to the chest while your lungs are full). Concentrate on taking regular breaths, and get in the habit of exhaling when your opponent strikes.

Blows to the Head

 Move into the punch to avoid head whipping.

If you sense a punch headed toward your skull, hold your ground. Even better, tighten your muscles and move toward it (this'll take some practice with a sparring partner). Pulling away from a punch only works if your opponent misses you completely. If you're hit while the head is moving backward, it can whip violently—leading to a knockout, concussion, or worse.

 Clench your jaw and tighten your neck muscles.

A stiff neck helps protect against the aforementioned head whipping, while a clenched jaw helps keep all those pearly whites in your mouth.

 Turn the other cheek.

If you absolutely, positively must get punched in the face, don't take it head-on. Instead, turn your face to the side so your jaw (tightly clenched, remember) takes the brunt of the blow. And whatever you do, protect that sniffer at all times. Getting hit in the nose is not only painful, it causes your eyes to water—and it's hard to fight when you can't see.

THE BEATING OF SPIDER-MAN'S LIFE

Acclaimed artist Todd McFarlane's first foray into writing Spider-Man, "Torment," is still one of the most discussed and debated Spider-Stories of all time. Dark and often ferocious, "Torment" pits Spidey against an old enemy: the Lizard. But McFarlane's Lizard is a hundred times more savage than earlier incarnations, and their ensuing battle (which spanned five issues) is arguably the most violent of the web-slinger's career. The saga begins with the Liz-Man on a killing spree, picking off citizens of New York City and tearing them apart. Naturally, Spidey has something to say about this, but during their first meeting, the Lizard poisons Spider-Man with his venomous claws. Spidey drags himself to the top of a water tower, reeling from the effects of the poison—but the Lizard is waiting for him. He hovers over the Arachknight's unconscious body, poised to slice his throat. But lucky (well, sort of) for Spider-Man, the Lizard is under the control of another villain, Calypso, who doesn't want our hero dead just yet. Instead, ol' Lizzy bone-crunchingly tosses Spidey's body down into an alley. The web-master wakes to find his hands bound, but he manages to escape and eventually launches a final showdown with the green machine. The Lizard knocks Spidey around like a cheap piñata, tearing chunks of flesh and shredding his costume with those razor-sharp teeth. And just when things can't get any worse, their battle ruptures a gas line, causing a devastating blast that levels the building they'd been fighting in. Blood-soaked, burned, and broken, Spidey finally manages to defeat the Lizard, but it's all he can do to crawl back to his apartment, where he pro-ceeds to sit on the bathroom floor and just bleed for a while.

Blunt Objects

■◘■ Protect your head.

Whether your opponent has a bat, crowbar, or bar stool, the goal is the same: Keep it away from your noggin at all costs. The most reliable method for protecting your *punim* is the classic boxer's stance: elbows perpendicular to the ground and fists out in front at chin level. Keep your eyes on the attacker, but pay attention to the periphery, too. Use your forearms to deflect strikes to the outside of your body.

■◘■ Block as close to the opponent's hands as possible.

When someone swings a bat, the tip is traveling much faster than the handle. So when you throw a block, throw it as close to your attacker's hands as possible.

■◘■ Avoid the middle ground.

When you're being chased with a steel rod, part of your brain (the wise part) gets on the horn and screams, "Run away!" And sometimes that's the best course of action. But if you have to make a stand against your blunt object–wielding foe, make sure you're always either very far away from the enemy (and well beyond the reach of whatever's being swung at you) or very close (and we mean right up against their body, robbing them of the leverage to get in a decent swing). Don't dance around at arm's length, or the enemy's liable to knock your head off the tee.

ALTERNATE METHOD: TAKE IT LYING DOWN

If you're knocked onto your back, you may want to consider staying there. No, that's not a dig at your fighting skills—it's merely a shift in strategy. Your legs are much stronger (and longer) than your arms, and thus able to absorb harder impacts at greater distances. Plus, since you're probably wearing shoes or boots, your feet are better suited to take a beating than your fragile hands and fingers. While lying on your back, use your legs to deflect the enemy's downward attacks, and counter by kicking him in the knees or groin whenever the opportunity presents itself.

How to Make Your Body a Weapon

Fantasy: You're a physically unspectacular specimen who gets bitten by a radioactive spider, thereby developing a rock-hard physique, extraordinary strength, and unparalleled endurance in a matter of minutes. Reality: You're a physically unspectacular specimen who spends more time blogging than jogging, and it's going to take some work to get you into super hero shape—especially if you want to be a crime fighter who (like Spider-Man) relies on strength and agility over weaponry.

Step 1: Make the necessary lifestyle changes.

It's time to surrender your party badge. Serving the public good requires a hero to sacrifice some of the bad—namely dropping any habits that could be detrimental to the body's effectiveness as a crime-fighting tool. You don't see Spider-Man doing keg stands, smoking cigarettes, drinking gallons of coffee, or eating chocolate fudge cake in the middle of the night. Wolverine maybe, but not Spidey. If your body is a temple, then you need to grab a mop and start scrubbing all the dirt you've tracked inside.

YOUR SUPER HERO GROCERY LIST

Buy:	Don't buy:
Fresh fruit	Cream-filled snack cakes
Sugar-free juice	Cola
Fresh vegetables	Microwavable frozen dinners
Rice	Whole milk
Whole-wheat pasta	Hot dogs

Step 2: Increase your stamina.

Imagine seeing Spidey lift up his mask and hurl on the sidewalk after running a block. It'd be downright embarrassing, not to mention gross. But barring the flu, it could never happen, because Spider-Man possesses incredible stamina. Therefore, the next step in becoming a human combat machine is making sure you have enough gas in the tank to get the job done. When you're locked in battle with an archcriminal, you don't get to hunch over and say, "Gimme a sec," no matter how badly your lungs burn or heart pounds. Some of the best ways to build cardiovascular and pulmonary endurance are jogging, jumping rope, and swimming. Chart your progress by keeping a log of your resting heart rate (it should gradually go down as your heart gets stronger) and timing how long it takes your breathing to return to normal after exercising.

Step 3: Increase your strength and agility.
Once you've removed the toxins from your diet and managed to run a mile (1.5 km) without puking, you can proceed to the next step: building some mass. Maintaining a well-toned, highly flexible body is crucial—yes, because of the obvious pugilistic advantages, but also for your self-confidence (would super heroes wear tights if they were embarrassed by their bodies?). Here's a four-prong attack for getting your muscles, joints, and ego into shape:

- Calisthenics: Crunches (three sets of 100), push-ups (three sets of 25), and pull-ups (three sets of 15).

- Weight training: If you're not an experienced weight lifter (and this book is the heaviest lifting you've done all day), have a professional trainer draw up a weight program for you—bench presses, bicep curls, leg curls, triceps extensions, etc.

- Yoga: All the muscles in the world won't do you any good if you can't move. Yoga builds strength while increasing flexibility to previously unimaginable levels.

- Gymnastics: Anyone who's seen Spidey in action knows the webbed one can hold his own against any gold-medal tumbler. As well as improving your balance and hand-eye coordination, knowing how to execute flips, tumbles, and vaults will serve you well in the field.

Step 4: Learn to ignore pain.
When the average human takes a right hook to the nose, the lightning bolt of pain makes it hard to stay focused—and in combat, a lack of focus can be fatal.

Through meditation, martial artists learn to control their breathing and ignore the pain until the fight is over.

Step 5: Develop your fighting skill.

By now, you should have strength, speed, endurance, and mental toughness in your arsenal. But in terms of technique, you're still just a blank canvas. Before you can go toe to toe with a super-villain, you'll need training. But rather than focus on a particular fighting style or martial art (just one of which could take decades to master) it's better to order up a "sampler platter" of disciplines. These five offer a healthy mix of defensive and offensive techniques:

- Aikido: This defensive martial art is designed to turn your opponent's energy against him through a combination of throws and joint locks. Great for close-quarters fighting.

- Boxing: Every fighter should know the basics of boxing—from breathing techniques to footwork to the best way to throw an uppercut. After all, despite the flips, kicks, and throws he's mastered, even Spider-Man can find himself in an old-fashioned street brawl once in a while.

- Jujitsu: The ancient art of hand-to-hand combat that was embraced by the samurai between the eighth and sixteenth centuries. Also a highly effective close-quarters art.

- Kung fu: This Chinese art can trace its roots back nearly 3,000 years. Although there are hundreds of variations, most of the basic styles of kung fu are based on animal movements.

- Savate: This discipline originated on the streets of nineteenth-century Paris, where men would fight by kicking each other with a *savate*, or "old shoe." Today, it's evolved into a full-fledged martial art, with a heavy emphasis on devastating kicks.

How to Survive an Electrical Assault

Villains love to use electricity as a weapon, whether it's a creepy galactic emperor shooting lightning from his fingertips or an ancient master barfing blue light in Little China. Spider-Man's no stranger to supercharged enemies, from lesser pests like Phreak to one of his oldest and most troublesome foes, Electro (see "Know Your Enemy," page 119). Point is, no matter what universe you inhabit, it's only a matter of time before somebody comes at you with an amp attack. And like Spidey, you'd better be ready when the sparks fly.

Alter your costume if necessary.
The wall-crawler once battled Electro wearing a Spider-Suit made from an old rubber mattress. Not quite state of the art, but it did the trick. If you don't have any bedding to spare, try these:

- **Fish paper:** A flexible, vulcanized fabric that's also an extraordinary electrical insulator (and yes, unfortunately named).

- **Class-four electrical gloves:** Worn for working on power lines, these rubber gloves are rated to handle up to 36,000 volts.

Before you head into battle, remove anything that might attract electricity: chains, bracelets, or loose change. You may also want to rethink those metal web-shooters. If you have a steel plate in your skull, well . . . good luck.

Don't stand your ground.
Electricity always takes the easiest path to the ground. And for us humans, the problem arises when we become part of that path. Being the science wiz that he is, Spidey knows that putting an insulator between his toes and the earth can help—but fighting with your feet on a fiberglass mat isn't exactly ideal. He also knows that air is a pretty good insulator. Therefore, when battling someone like Electro, he stays airborne as much as possible.

Deploy metal chaff.

In military terms, *chaff* describes the small pieces of aluminum that planes release to confuse enemy radars. The same technique can also confuse the enemy's bolts of electricity. As you bounce all over the place (keep those feet off the ground, remember), toss conductive bits and pieces in the air to draw fire. In the absence of chaff, use your surroundings as a shield—whether it's ducking behind radio towers or crouching behind a city bus.

Soak your opponent to cause a short circuit.

If there's one thing electrical villains can't stand, it's water (makes you wonder how Electro smells, since he can't shower). So get your opponent wet by any means necessary, whether it's a garden hose or a water balloon (Spidey's been known to crack open a few fire hydrants). But be warned: As the enemy snaps, crackles, and pops, don't touch any part of the puddle he's standing in, lest you become the world's crispiest crime fighter.

Strike with nonconductive weapons.

Good idea: hitting your opponent with wood, rubber, and fiberglass. Bad idea: hitting your opponent with aluminum bats, crowbars, and car antennas. Horrible idea: licking your opponent (this also applies to nonelectrical foes).

Drain your opponent's energy.

Since the opponent's source of electricity is probably exhaustible, the more shots you get him to take, the less energy he'll have to fry you with. When facing Electro, Spider-Man tries to draw as much fire as possible, knowing every shot will be a little weaker than the last.

Once the enemy's electrical reserves are gone, hit him on the head.

Container of metal chaff

Fish paper

Class 4
electrical gloves

Wooden bat

Water pistol

KNOW YOUR ENEMY: ELECTRO

Name: Maxwell Dillon
First Appearance: *Amazing Spider-Man* #8 (1964)
Height and Weight: 5'11" (180 cm), 165 pounds (75 kg)
Powers: Abilities to generate up to a million volts of electricity, "fly" along
electrical wires, and manipulate electrical devices with his mind

Even before he became a super-criminal, Max Dillon was a pretty despicable
guy. He was the electric company's best lineman, but when one of his cowork-
ers was electrocuted and left hanging from a utility pole, Dillon demanded a
hundred-dollar bonus before shimmying up to rescue him. In a textbook defini-
tion of instant karma, he was struck by lightning during the rescue. But instead
of killing him, the lightning gave Max incredible powers over electricity.

His body now acted as a power generator, creating and storing electricity
at the rate of 1,000 volts per minute, with a 100,000-volt maximum. He could
shoot bolts of electricity from his fingertips that'd kill a person at ten feet (3 m),
and manipulate electrical devices with his mind. He could also "fly" along
power lines at 140 miles per hour (225 km/h) and, in some cases, make
"bridges" of electricity to walk across (but this used up a lot of juice). Dillon
adopted the name "Electro" and fashioned himself a (rather flamboyant) costume. He may have had a new persona, but he was the same greedy rapscallion who wanted a bribe to save a life. So naturally, his first order of criminal
business was a bank heist. This drew the attention of Spider-Man, who made
short work of the volt-happy villain. Embarrassed, Electro was now a proud
member of the "I hereby swear to take my revenge by killing Spider-Man"
club and joined forces with the Sinister Six—a band of his fellow disgruntled
Spider-Enemies (including Doctor Octopus and the Sandman).

Electro's been a thorn (or a spark, if you will) in Spidey's side ever since.
J. J. Jameson once hired him to battle Spider-Man on national television
(Spidey won). He tried to drain Manhattan's power (he almost died, and
Spidey had to save his life). He also suffered defeat at the hands of Captain
America, Daredevil, and the Fantastic Four. You'd think that after so many
beatings, Max Dillon would hang up his batteries for good. But greed con-
quers all, and so long as there's a buck to be stolen, Electro will be working
on a plan to steal it.

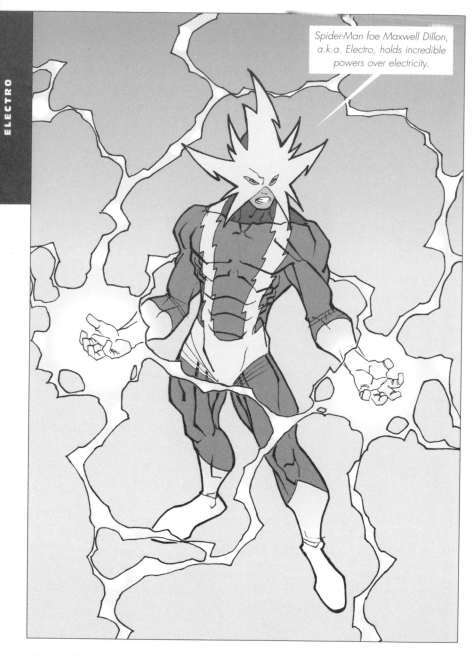

Spider-Man foe Maxwell Dillon, a.k.a. Electro, holds incredible powers over electricity.

How to Crash Through a Window

Peter Parker has it all wrong. The perfect line of work for a super hero's alter ego? Glass repair. Think about it: As a masked crime fighter, you're always making pane-shattering high-rise escapes and throwing crooks through windows. And how many times has some maniac thrown a bus down Sixth Avenue and taken out half a block of storefront glass? That alone would generate enough business to pay for a year's worth of Mary Jane's acting lessons! What a wonderful world it would be. Spider Man would break it, and Panes by Parker would conveniently show up the next morning to fix it. Pete would virtually have a license to print money, and he'd never have to cross paths with J. J. Jameson again (see "How to Deal with a Nightmare Boss," page 167). Alas, until that beautiful day, the only thing Spider-Man will gain from crashing though a window is a few cuts. You, however, could *lose* quite a bit more—a limb, for instance—if you're not careful.

Step 1: Get a running start.

Yes, you're a hero—but don't *be* a hero. If there's time, pick up a heavy object (an office chair, for instance) and use it to break the glass first. But if a bomb is seconds away from detonating, or if the building's about to collapse, then by all means, crash away. Start by gaining plenty of momentum. Some industrial glass can be up to $3/4$ inch (19 mm) thick, in which case nothing short of an all-out sprint will be enough to break it.

Step 2: Protect your face and neck.

Close your hands into fists (no need to sever a finger), and bring them up in front of your face, like a boxer blocking an onslaught of punches. Next, shrug your shoulders so they cover the sides of your neck.

Step 3: Aim for the center of the window.

The farther glass is from the frame, the easier it is to break.

Step 4: Lead with your shoulder or forearm.

If you're in an older or residential building (an abandoned warehouse or private home), your forearms might be strong enough to do the trick—especially if you're wearing those trusty metal web-shooters on your wrists. But if you're in an industrial building (an office tower or store), you can safely assume the glass you'll be crashing through is tempered, and it's best to lead with your shoulder. In either case, keep your head down.

Step 5: Launch.

This is no time for half measures. If you hesitate before the moment of impact, you run the risk of bouncing off the glass, or worse—getting caught in a rain of falling shards. Forget the fact that you're running *into* something. Instead, visualize yourself running *through* it.

Step 6: Keep your eyes closed, whether you're wearing a mask or not.

If this doesn't happen instinctively, you may want to consider another line of work.

Step 7: Brush or shake the glass off before you do anything else.

Once you've cleared the window frame and, in some cases, survived plummeting 50 stories back to Earth (see "How to Survive Falling from a Tall Building," page 82), you'll find yourself covered in tiny pieces of broken glass. Keep your eyes closed, and brush off your face and neck before resuming your crime-fighting activities.

TYPES OF GLASS

- **Untempered:** What you probably think of as "plain" glass. It has the unfortunate tendency to break into big, jagged, flesh-slicing shards. Used mostly in residential windows.

- **Tempered:** Tempered or "safety" glass is heat treated, giving it greater strength (about four times that of untempered glass). By design, tempered glass breaks into hundreds of tiny pieces when it shatters, greatly reducing (but not eliminating) the risk of severe injury. Used in office buildings, cars, shower doors, and more.

- **Laminated:** Another type of "safety" glass (actually a thin sheet of plastic sandwiched between two pieces of glass). It's used in many of the same applications as tempered glass, most often in car windshields. The glass tends to cling to the plastic layer upon impact, making it very difficult to shatter.

Chapter 4

Law Enforcement Skills

"You see, but you do not observe."
—Sherlock Holmes

If you're getting into the super hero business for action and adventure, prepare to be sorely disappointed. Sure, there'll be battles, explosions, and trips to strange alternate dimensions, but the other 99 percent of your time will be spent gathering evidence, conducting surveillance, and consulting law books. If you want action and adventure, try archaeology . . .

How to Pick a Criminal Out of a Crowd

Crime fighters like Spider-Man don't rent themselves out as personal body-guards, but occasionally they'll volunteer their services for the right person. Say the mayor is hosting a big political rally and city officials are worried about his safety. This opportunity is too good to refuse—you'll be preventing crime *and* boosting your rep at City Hall. Here's the catch: The job will require you to spot threats before they materialize. It's a skill that'll serve you well, whether you're babysitting a VIP or simply going about your plain-clothes life. With some help from former Secret Service special agent Brian Helbing, here's a guide to spotting nefarious ne'er-do-wells.

Be alert for alertness.
The next time you're out in public, take note of how many people pay absolutely no attention to what's going on around them. Generally speaking, there are two types of people who take note of their surroundings (when getting out of a car or walking into a lobby, for instance): cops and crooks. The rest of the population seems to have tunnel vision. Therefore, if you notice someone being especially attentive—looking over their shoulder or scanning their surroundings—they may be a threat.

Look for unconscious adjustments.
Most criminals don't use holsters for their guns, so as they walk (especially going up and down curbs or stairs) they'll tend to unconsciously grab the weapon to keep it in place.

Look for outward signs of anxiety.
When most people get close to a dignitary (like the president) they're bug-eyed with excitement, smiling ear to ear, and reaching out in hopes of touching a piece of living history. Either that, or they're fumbling with a disposable camera. So if someone looks especially serious, focused, or worried—if they're sweating a bit too much, or they're fidgety—that person deserves your utmost attention. This

applies to your daily life, too: Someone who's about to commit a robbery or violent assault is usually chock full of adrenaline, and might display symptoms like heavy breathing, hard swallowing, trembling hands, and dilated pupils.

▰◖▸ Watch the hands.

No matter how ugly, no matter how sinister or menacing, a facial expression never killed anybody. When the president works a "rope line" (a barrier that keeps the crowd back), his bodyguards constantly order onlookers to take their hands out of their pockets. Until people learn to shoot guns with their toes, hands should always be your first concern—whether you're protecting a VIP in your costume or waiting in line at the bank in your street clothes.

DON'T BE A SEXIST SUPER HERO

Women typically account for 15 percent of violent criminals, but that's no reason to ignore them. There have been plenty of dangerous damsels throughout history:

- **Aileen Wuornos** was a serial killer who murdered seven men in Florida.

- **Lynette "Squeaky" Fromme** pointed a .45 pistol at President Gerald Ford in 1975.

- **Bonnie Parker**, half of the murderous Bonnie and Clyde, was a cold-blooded killer.

- **Lizzie Borden** famously "took an axe" and gave her parents "forty whacks" with it.

- **Grace O'Malley** was a sixteenth-century Irish noblewoman, pirate, and vicious warrior.

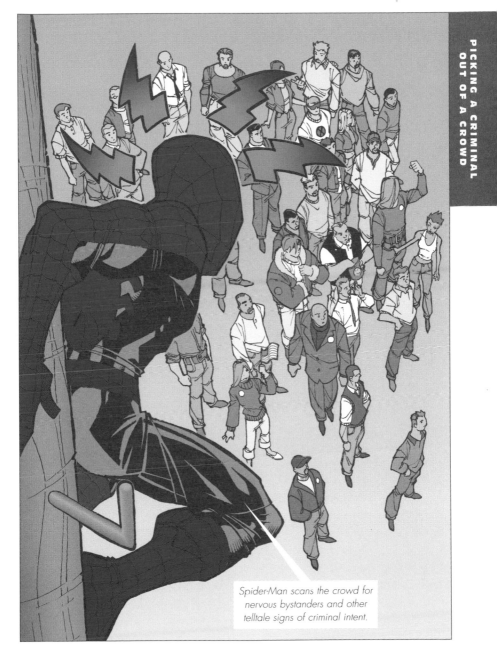

Spider-Man scans the crowd for nervous bystanders and other telltale signs of criminal intent.

How to Negotiate the Release of a Hostage

Sometimes it's a premeditated political statement. Sometimes it's the last resort of a desperate criminal. And sometimes, it's just a cry for help. But regardless of its origins, every hostage crisis has the same conclusion: It either ends very well (surrender and safe recovery of the hostages) or very badly (murder, suicide, or both). The web-slinger has faced tense hostage standoffs, and unfortunately, the outcomes haven't always been bloodless (see "Spider-Man's Hostage Situations," page 132). But with some basic knowledge of negotiation techniques, you might be able to avoid an equally grim conclusion. How you handle yourself will determine whether innocent lives are saved or tragically cut short.

No pressure.

Step 1: Evacuate the area.

The hostage taker could open fire or detonate a bomb at any moment. To minimize the risk of injury to innocent bystanders from shrapnel or stray bullets, clear one square block around the house or building in question (hopefully, the police will arrive quickly to help close the streets to cars and pedestrians).

Step 2: Place yourself in the hostage taker's frame of mind.

Dismissing the suspect as a madman is easy, but that'll hurt your ability to negotiate. Before you make contact, remind yourself how stressed and frightened he must be. Most hostage takers believe that the police are eager to take a shot at them, and that (no matter what) they'll spend the rest of their lives in jail. It's vital that you address these fears right off the bat and put them (even slightly) at ease. It's also vital that you focus on staying as calm as possible.

Step 3: Research the suspect.

If any of the suspect's friends or relatives are nearby, quickly get as much information as you can. Does he have a history of mental illness? Is he having trouble at work (layoffs)? Marital or domestic problems? Husbands and boyfriends will often take their own children hostage in the wake of a fight with their wives or girlfriends. In these cases, it's best to keep her far away from the negotiations, for fear that her mere presence could further enrage him.

Step 4: Open a line of communication, and demonstrate concern for the hostage taker's welfare.
Whether you have to talk with a phone, a bullhorn, or even through a door, establish communication with the hostage taker in a calm, nonthreatening manner. Open by asking if he is okay (stupid question, yes—but effective).

Step 5: Avoid saying "hostage" at all costs.
The suspect's already under a great deal of stress. Hearing the word *hostage* only serves to remind him of the seriousness of the situation (and the potential consequences). After asking if the hostage taker is okay, ask if "the others" need medical attention.

Step 6: Establish trust.
You want the suspect to see you as an ally—you and him against the world. Ask if he needs anything, but don't surrender your authority. For instance, give him water, but only if he promises to share it with the others. Give him cigarettes, but only one or two at a time (that way, he'll have to ask for more, and you'll get to "reward" him more frequently).

Step 7: When in doubt, blame someone else.
If there's something you *can't* give him (a gallon of gas, a bazooka, any combination thereof), then by all means, tell the suspect that those "no good, by-the-book cops" or "pencil-necked city hall types" wouldn't authorize it.

Step 8: Keep the suspect talking.
Hostage negotiation is a war of attrition. He who waits it out the longest usually wins (which, consequently, is why the hostage taker never wins—since the police control resources like food and electricity). The more you keep the suspect talking, the more tired he'll get, and the less focused he'll be on the hostages inside (and dozens of police revolvers outside). Stressed out and deprived of sleep, the suspect's focus and determination will slowly erode.

Step 9: Ask the hostage taker to come up with a solution.

Reinforce the trust and "mutual respect" you've established by asking the hostage taker to offer up his version of a solution. Assure him that you're doing everything you can to make sure each and every demand is met, but that it would really help the cause if he'd make a gesture of good faith, such as releasing one of the others.

Step 10: Make sure the suspect knows that if a hostage is hurt or killed, all bets are off.

Calmly remind him that there's nothing you'll be able to do to hold back the cops if something unfortunate befalls one of the others.

Step 11: If shots are fired, immediately demand proof of life.

If the hostage taker doesn't *immediately* comply with this demand, storm the castle.

SPIDER-MAN'S HOSTAGE SITUATIONS

Spidey's faced tense hostage situations on more than one occasion.

"A House Divided"

Aunt May and some of her boarders are taken hostage by four miserable miscreants. With police surrounding May's house, Spider-Man enters and knocks them out one by one—except for the ringleader, who's shot and killed by a police sniper.

"Carnage, Part 1"

A group of innocents is held in a Brooklyn building by an exceptionally tall suspect who demands the liberation of another foe, Emperor Nurhachi. But Spidey takes him down and saves the day.

"Countdown"

Doctor Octopus holds a Palestinian foreign minister hostage, throwing the Middle East into turmoil and sending the world to the brink of war. His sole demand? That Spider-Man remove his mask in the middle of Times Square. Spidey cleverly complies by peeling off his mask to reveal a second mask, enraging Doc Ock and sparking a ferocious battle which (you guessed it) Spidey eventually wins.

How to Process a Crime Scene

You decide to pay a visit to one of the local lowlifes—a petty thief who might have some information on the whereabouts of your archnemesis. But when you show up at his seedy apartment, the door's already open, and all the lights are out. You enter cautiously, Spider-Sense tingling off the hook. It doesn't take a supersleuth to know that something bad has happened here. But what? And when? And most importantly, who did it? Processing a crime scene requires a strict adherence to certain procedures: They're designed to make sure the investigator (in this case, you) leaves no stone unturned, and a failure to follow them could come back to haunt you in the courtroom. If you don't fancy the thought of solving a crime only to see it tossed out on a technicality, pay attention.

Step 1:   Secure the scene.
First things first—make sure the bad guy isn't lurking in the shadows waiting to get the drop on you. Then (once you've determined that the perpetrator is long gone), make sure no one else wanders into your crime scene and disturbs the evidence. Whether indoors or out, shoot web lines around the perimeter. This serves the dual purpose of keeping unwanted onlookers from getting too close and alerting the police to your presence when they arrive (it's never a good idea to surprise cops when they're responding to a crime).

Step 2:   Don't touch *anything* . . .
. . . unless you absolutely have to. And even then, use a latex glove or handkerchief to handle it.

Step 3:   Determine the nature of the crime.
Just because there's a blood-soaked body lying at your feet doesn't mean you've stumbled onto a murder. And just because the scene is sans corpse doesn't mean you haven't. Avoid jumping to early conclusions. Yes, maybe there's a body—but maybe it's a suicide, or a burglary gone wrong. Maybe the victim killed the

perpetrator and ran away in a panic, and you're standing over the corpse of a criminal. Assuming the crime scene is indoors, keep an open mind as you look for points of entry, such as distressed door frames and broken windows. Search for signs of a struggle—things like dented drywall, broken knickknacks, and bullet holes. In private homes, check bedrooms and studies to see if someone's gone through dressers or desks. Check the kitchen garbage for discarded blood-soaked paper towels and cleaning products, as these could be signs that a body has been moved elsewhere.

Step 4: Photograph the scene.
Taking care not to disturb the evidence, take photographs of everything in sight, starting with the body (if there is one) and any objects around it. Be sure to get a mix of wide shots (the layout of the room), close-ups (knives, pry marks) and extreme close-ups (pupils, blood drops). You never know which seemingly "unimportant" detail could break the case wide open, so don't overlook anything—no matter how innocuous it appears. When shooting close-ups, place a ruler in the frame for size reference.

Step 5: Collect physical evidence.
In the case of a murder, the body is the single most important piece of physical evidence. Are there bullet wounds? Strangulation marks? Signs of blunt trauma? Does the victim have anything under his or her fingernails (perhaps even bits of the attacker's skin)? After examining the body (if one is present), look for anything the criminal might've unwittingly left behind. This includes footprints, clothing fibers, hairs, handwriting samples, shell casings, cigarette butts, dirt, and drops of blood—anything that could link the perpetrator to the scene.

Step 6: Dust for fingerprints.
Fingerprint kits are readily available to the public, and usually include silk black latent powder, a camel hair brush, latex gloves, white backing cards, and clear lifting tape. Start by dipping your brush into the latent powder and wiping it over surfaces that you suspect might hold fingerprints. If a print does appear, press a piece of clear lifting tape over it and peel it off. Then stick the clear tape over a white backing card and examine away.

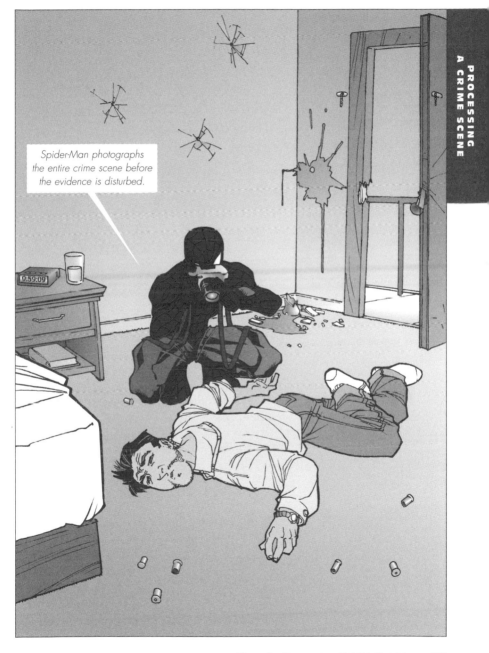

Spider-Man photographs the entire crime scene before the evidence is disturbed.

Step 7: Share your findings with the authorities.

Even though you've taken great care not to disturb any of the evidence, you've probably left traces of your own presence. And unless you feel like being wrongfully indicted for the crime you're investigating, be sure to let the police in on your findings. Besides, sharing evidence is the super-heroic thing to do. You're all on the same team, right?

Right?

FIVE TIPS FOR BETTER CRIME SCENE PHOTOGRAPHS

Spider-Man is the reigning shutterbug of the super hero world (when your secret identity makes his living as a photographer, you'd better be). And it's safe to assume that his crime scene photos would rival any professional's. But if you're among the photographically challenged, keep these tips in mind:

- **Use a 50mm lens:** This will give your pictures the same field of vision as the human eye.

- **Go digital:** This allows you to review your photos and spot any duds before leaving the scene. You'll also be able to examine your snaps the instant you get to a computer.

- **Use a flash:** Save the artsy stuff for later. You want a bright, evenly lit picture—and a flash is the quickest way to get it.

- **Shoot from eye level:** When photographing the layout of a room (or the position of a body), try to shoot from eye level as much as possible. This is the angle most people (including jurors) are accustomed to seeing.

- **Keep your lens clean:** The slightest smudge or speck on your lens could spell disaster in the courtroom.

How to Make and Plant a Tracking Device

The ad would go something like this: "Archnemesis give you the slip again? Tired of all-night stakeouts that turn up zilch? Well don't waste another minute! Announcing the Spider-Tracer! A revolutionary tool for *today's* super hero—the super hero who balances crime fighting with a busy schedule of carpooling, work, soccer practice, doctor's appointments, grocery shopping, and more!"

It didn't take Spider-Man long to amass a small army of enemies, and it didn't take Peter Parker long to realize he'd go nuts trying to keep tabs on all of them. So, when Doc Ock was released from prison (the first time), Petey came up with an ingenious way to track his whereabouts: a microtransmitter shaped like an itsy-bitsy spider (actually, early models weren't so "itsy-bitsy"—but back then, a "chip" was something you ate), complete with "aerodynamic" legs for accurate throwing and adhesive coating. Through the years, they've proven effective at uncovering secret hideouts, snagging slippery villains, and yes—luring Spidey into a trap or two . . . or ten.

Construct a tiny, motion-activated, all-weather, spider-shaped, battery-powered, active GPS tracking unit.

Describing each step would be insulting to your intelligence. Suffice it to say, you'll be able to knock one of these puppies out in a matter of minutes. Just make sure it's encased in a weatherproof shell, small enough to be hidden in clothing, and includes an active GPS antenna. "Active" GPS units send location updates every few seconds, while "passive" units store a bunch of location data and send a big update once or twice a day. That's fine for studying migration patterns of east African wildebeests, but not so helpful for tracking a criminal to his secret hideout in real time. For longer battery life, make the device motion activated.

 Tune your GPS antenna to 1575.42 MHz—the frequency open to civilians. The U.S. Department of Defense developed the global positioning system but allows free civilian access.

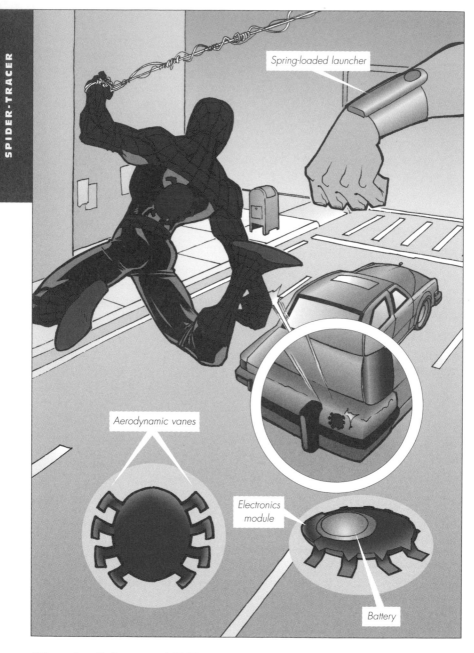

SPIDER-TRACER

Spring-loaded launcher

Aerodynamic vanes

Electronics module

Battery

▨▨▨ Rig up a mobile monitoring device.

Early spider-tracers were tracked with a handheld transistor radio, but later, the webster tuned them to his Spider-Sense, eliminating the need for a portable receiver. Cool, but not in the cards for you. You'll need some kind of portable device to keep track of your tracer's signal. Converting a PDA, smart phone, or preexisting GPS unit is probably the easiest way (again, this should be no problem and take only a matter of minutes to accomplish). But for you purists out there—you super heroes who absolutely must have 100 percent custom gear—you'll want the monitor to be small, lightweight, and equipped with an organic LED screen (organic LEDs are lighter, brighter, and use less power than traditional LEDs). You'll also want some kind of expansion or communication port for archiving data on another computer and uploading new maps if you travel abroad.

▨▨▨ Plant the spider-tracer.

- On a vehicle: In a pinch, just throw the thing and hope for the best. But if there's time, plant your tracer under one of the car's bumpers—where it's less likely to be seen, and where it won't get damaged by moving or hot parts of the undercarriage. Like Peter's prototype, your spider-tracers should be coated with a strong adhesive. Unless car manufacturers bring back the good old days of metal bumpers, magnets won't work on the foam-filled fiberglass fronts and backs of modern cars.

- On a person: If possible, plant the device in advance (the underside of hats, heels of shoes, and linings of coats are always reliable). But if you don't have access to the suspect's wardrobe, try the ol' "bump 'n' plant." Using your civilian identity, arrange to "accidentally" bump into the suspect in a crowded elevator or subway car. Politely excuse yourself for being so clumsy, and privately congratulate yourself for being so clever.

SPIDER-MAN'S TRACKING FOLLIES

Handy as they are, spider-tracers haven't always led the Arachknight down the right path:

"Web of Confusion, Part 1"

Spider-Man is tracking Sleepwalker, an alien who's trapped in the mind of a human host, Rick (and can only materialize when Rick's asleep). Spidey plants a tracer on Sleepwalker, but when the alien vanishes into Rick's unconscious, the tracer falls to the floor and gets eaten by Rick's dog, Rambo. The next day, Spidey tracks the signal to the belly of a confused canine.

"Hobgoblin Lives, Part 3"

The hostage-taking Hobgoblin discovers a pair of tracers on his person and sees an opportunity to throw Spider-Man off his trail. It works. Spidey follows one signal to a homeless woman and chases down an unsuspecting cyclist (whose bicycle has been tagged with the other tracer) before realizing he's been had.

"The Other: Evolve or Die, Part 1"

While chasing a villain named Tracer (oh, sweet irony!), Spidey tracks the signal to a moving limo. Convinced that his enemy is inside, he stops the car, rips the roof open, and pulls out . . . J. J. Jameson? Peter Parker's boss and notorious Spider-Man detractor J. J. Jameson? Oh, crap. Spidey sums it up perfectly, saying, "Well . . . this is bad on just so many levels."

How to Trail a Criminal Without Being Detected

Spider-Man would make a world-class spy, if for no other reason than his ability to follow people undetected. He can scurry along walls, rooftops, and ceilings without making a sound, he can travel high above the city streets without casting a shadow, and he has perfect vision, day or night. When he's on your tail, there's no shaking him (not that you'd know he was there in the first place). Your new line of work will require you to track down secret headquarters, tail suspected villains—even tail friends and loved ones for their own protection. And since using a spider-tracer won't always be an option, it's in your best interest to memorize the following spy techniques. You may want to try reading them over your shoulder.

Establish a chokepoint.
In spy circles, a chokepoint is a location you know the subject (called a rabbit) has to pass through. It could be the lobby of an office building, a parking garage, or the front door of her duplex. It's also where you'll wait—patiently and indiscreetly—for her to emerge.

Alter your appearance.
Avoid wearing brightly colored or distinctive clothing (sorry—the red and blue tights won't cut it this time). Carry a couple of hats and a pair of sunglasses with you, too (especially if you know the rabbit). As you follow her, change your look by alternating between hat, no hat, glasses, no glasses, and so on.

Recruit a pair of spider-pals.
Professional spies prefer to tail a rabbit in groups of three. Recruit a pair of friends, and equip yourselves with radios and earpieces to stay in communication. Assign one person to be the lead (called the eye) and follow closest to the rabbit. A second person should follow directly behind her and be ready to take the lead if anything should happen. The third tail follows on the other side of the street and is prepared to take over if the suspect suddenly crosses or doubles back.

Never, ever, ever make eye contact with the rabbit.

If you do, consider yourself "burned." That's spy lingo for "you're busted."

Don't get close, and don't get frustrated.

When following on foot, stay as far away from rabbits as possible, and don't speed up when you lose them around corners (if they double back, you're burned). If you lose them altogether, don't draw attention to yourself by frantically looking in every direction. Live to tail another day. Remember: If you're trying to locate a secret hideout, then the rabbit will be back this way again. Go back to your chokepoint and try again.

If your rabbit gets in a cab . . .

Forget everything you've seen in the movies. Real spies don't hop in conveniently parked cabs and say, "Follow that car." First of all, good luck finding *one* available cab in Midtown, let alone *two* right next to each other. Second, most cab drivers don't want anything to do with covert chases and will probably kick you out of the car. If your rabbit hails a cab, note the company name and car number. Track it down later, and bribe the driver to fork over the rabbit's destination.

If an Archcriminal Is Following You

As a super hero, you have a lot of enemies. And eventually (no matter how smart you are), one of them will begin to suspect your secret identity. If the trailing tables are turned, it's better to be paranoid than dead.

Check your six without turning around.

If you think you're being followed, stay calm. Don't break into an all-out sprint or turn around and yell "gotcha!" just yet. First of all, people will think you're crazy. Second, if you *are* being tailed, it could provoke a confrontation that doesn't need to happen. Calmly walk to the nearest street level window. As you pass it, casually look in the reflection and see what you can make out behind you.

Pull a "Crazy Ivan."

In Tom Clancy's *The Hunt for Red October*, Russian sub commanders would unexpectedly turn their ships to see if anyone was following them in a maneuver nicknamed the Crazy Ivan. If you're being followed, try turning around abruptly, as if you've forgotten something. When you do, take note of anyone who suddenly looks away or seems startled.

Try the ol' subway slip.
If you're near a subway station, get to it fast. When the train arrives, make like you're going to get on, but hesitate at the last second and stay on the platform. Your tail now has two choices: get on the train, or blow his cover.

Peter Parker uses a store window to study his reflection.

Peter uses the ol' "subway slip" to foil a goon.

How to Indemnify Yourself Against Legal Action

Let's be crystal clear: By donning a mask and taking crime fighting into his own hands, Spider-Man's already in violation of who knows how many laws. Be thankful the cops like him, because legally speaking, there's nothing keeping them from tossing Spidey in the slammer next to the scum he's swept off the streets (although they'd have to catch him first). As a super hero, you'll deal with situations that can lead to massive property damage, serious physical and emotional injury, and even loss of life—and that's on a slow day. And while you can't be hauled into court as long as you retain your anonymity, you could face billions of dollars in civil lawsuits if your secret identity is ever revealed. That is, unless you take steps to protect yourself from winding up on the wrong side of a verdict.

Create a liability shield.

Your first experience with liability shields probably came in grade school, when you were sent home with permission slips for a parent's signature (thus indemnifying the school when you fell into a vat of boiling acid on the battery factory field trip). Later in life, you may have signed a presurgical waiver acknowledging that the procedure could kill you, or gone to a theme park, where the backs of tickets are covered in volumes of fine print. In legalese, it's known as "covering one's butt." So before you swing into action, sit down with an attorney and type up a release of liability document, which might look something like this:

I, [CITIZEN'S NAME], ("Citizen") being of sound mind and body, acknowledge that I am over the age of majority and have the right to contract in my own name, and release, discharge, and covenant not to sue the professional crime fighter known to the public as "[YOUR SUPER HERO NAME]" ("Super Hero"). Further, I fully understand that being in the immediate vicinity of Super Hero involves serious risks, including—but not limited to—bodily injury, disability, accidental genetic mutation into a quasihuman criminal lunatic, and death. I have read this agreement and understand it to be a complete and unconditional release of all liability, and have received no inducements to sign it. This agreement shall be binding against my heirs, attorneys, administrators, executors, and assigns, throughout this and alternate universes, in perpetuity.

Signed _____ Date _____

Don't leave home without blank copies and a pen.

Incorporate.

As an individual, everything you own is vulnerable to a lawsuit: your bank accounts, your home, your car—even your future earnings. Therefore, it's in a super hero's best interest to set up a limited liability corporation (LLC) to protect his personal assets. If Peter Parker ever decided to go corporate, he'd start by hiring one of the many professional services that guide individuals through the process. Together, they'd pick a name (perhaps "Sticky Solutions LLC") and choose a state to file in (Delaware and Nevada have America's most favorable corporate statutes). Peter would then be listed as one of the company's employees and given the job description of "crime fighter." If anyone ever discovered his identity and sued him for damages, she'd be forced to sue a company with virtually no assets, instead of a financially shaky newspaper photographer.

Carry business liability insurance.

To further protect yourself from paying out of pocket in the event of a lawsuit, have your LLC insured. Yes, you'll have to pay a monthly premium, but if your company is dragged to court, at least all those exorbitant legal fees will be covered.

Wear disclaimers on your costume.

Ever notice how many warnings you get in a day? Watch a car commercial, and you'll see those incredibly tiny words at the bottom of the screen: "Professional driver on closed course," and so on. Walk on a freshly mopped floor, and you'll see that good old yellow sign warning that you're about to slip and break your neck. In today's ultralitigious world, reminders of the obvious are everywhere, so why should your costume be any different? Try adding highly visible disclaimers to the front and back of your duds: "Caution! Super hero at work—keep back 500 ft!" "Danger! Falling villain zone!" "Warning! Do not eat webbing!"

Know your legal limitations.

If Spider-Man detains a suspect, he'd better have a good reason—and he'd better turn that person over to the police as quickly as possible. Failure to do so would constitute a "false arrest," leading to the charges being dropped and opening the door to a lawsuit against the web-slinger. As a vigilante (albeit a well-meaning one) never forget that you have no actual law enforcement powers. Legally speaking, your rights are the same as any ordinary person's. That is, if you witness someone committing a crime, you have the right to place that person under citizen's arrest (use of reasonable force to detain her) until the police arrive.

KNOW YOUR MIRANDA RIGHTS

In 1966, the U.S. Supreme Court issued a ruling in the case of *Miranda v. Arizona*, which stated that all suspects have the right to remain silent and the right to competent legal representation, and that their statements can't be used as evidence until they've been advised of those rights. Since then, police have been required to read the Miranda Rights to anyone they arrest:

You have the right to remain silent. Anything you say can and will be used against you in a court of law. You have the right to have an attorney present during questioning. If you cannot afford an attorney, one will be appointed to you free of charge at your request. Do you understand these rights?

How to Force a Thug to Fess Up

If a university offered Super Hero as a major, it would be heavy on drama and psychology classes. Drama because—let's face it—being a masked crime fighter is about as theatrical as it gets. And psychology because, when it comes to solving crimes and saving the day, you're often called upon to interrogate some pretty unsavory characters. Forget the bright lights and two-way mirrors. Forget the tape recorders and pitchers of water. When Spidey needs information, he doesn't have the luxury of dragging a suspect downtown—and he doesn't have time to play games (ditto for you on both counts). Over the years, he's become a highly skilled (and speedy) interrogator—not through intimidation or violence, but through psychological interrogation techniques. Sometimes, words are more powerful than weapons . . .

Step 1: Remember: It's not what you know, it's what they *think* you know. Act as if you've got it all figured out and that you're simply humoring the thug by letting him tell his side of the story. When he offers up details, smirk (unless your mouth is covered by a mask, in which case, start every sentence with "Pardon my smirk, but . . .") and say things like, "So that's what you're going with?" And, "Are you sure? Because that's not what people are saying."

Step 2: Start with "hypothetical empathy."
Ease the suspect into feeling comfortable by identifying with their motives. "Listen, Rocco. I'm not saying you're the one who killed Frankie—but if you *were*, I'd understand. He was a bad guy. He had it coming, and whoever gave it to him probably deserves a medal."

Step 3: Throw a few curveballs.
Keep the suspect off guard (and less defensive) by changing your line of questioning to include subjects relevant to the case and subjects that are totally unrelated. "What time did you eat at that restaurant again?" "You see the Yanks last night? Man, what's going on with that bullpen?" If you're lucky, this non-sequitur

approach will lead the thug to slip up. "Wait, if you saw the Yanks play, how could you have been at the restaurant that late?"

Step 4: Make the accusation.
After you've worn him down with implied knowledge, hypothetical empathy, and curveball questions, go ahead and take your shot. Tell the thug you "know" he did it. All you want to know is, why? "Help me understand. Was it revenge? Money? Self-defense? Did he want you dead?" Look the suspect in the eye—let him know you're confident in what you're saying.

Step 5: Remind the thug what's at stake.
Namely jail time, and lots of it. In the same breath, remind him that you have a lot of pull with the D.A. and the cops, and that you could go a long way to seeing that he's given leniency—if he cooperates. And if that doesn't work, remind him that you could just as easily go to his boss (probably a super-villain) and put the word out that there's a rat in the organization.

Step 6: Only use the threat of violence as a last resort.
If you were a 1930s-era private eye, you'd let this piker know that you're no palooka and that he was about to hear a little chin music played on his puss. But thankfully, you're not, so there's no need to make yourself sound like an idiot. Simply pick the thug up and carry him to the top of the tallest building in sight and offer him a unique view of the sidewalk (see "How to Strike Fear into Your Enemies," page 43).

If You're Being Interrogated

Spider-Man has spent more time on the grill than most short-order cooks. And when he's under the lights, it's safe to assume that the interrogator isn't a badge-wielding detective and that he's not being questioned in a "comfy" police precinct. But even when he's tied up in a subterranean dungeon getting questioned by a raving psycho, the webbed one always keeps his cool.

Stay in your happy place.
Be as dispassionate as possible, even if you're scared to death (but don't be too detached, as this could be taken as a sign of defensiveness). And don't lash out

Spider-Man tries desperately to "stay in a happy place."

angrily, no matter how much you're provoked. Remember: You're a super hero. This is *nothing*.

■◗◖■ Keep your answers short and sweet.
This is a tough one. You should answer as succinctly as possible, but not so succinctly that you come off as evasive. On the other hand, giving too many details can be a sign of a made-up story. If the interrogator asks, "How many people were at the party?" don't answer, "Thirty-one," and proceed to name them all. Simply say, "I don't know . . . twenty? Maybe more, I can't remember."

■◗◖■ Refuse to answer unrelated questions.
Don't fall for your own "curveball" technique. If the interrogator asks you, "Man, you see the Yanks last night?" simply say, "I don't see how that has anything to do with the case." Then, prepare to get punched in the face for being such a smart-mouth (see "How to Withstand a Savage Beating," page 108).

■◗◖■ Don't give off any "tells."
These include nonverbal cues such as shifting your position, slouching, completely avoiding eye contact, and crossing your arms or legs.

■◗◖■ Proclaim your innocence.
Police detectives know that only a guilty person sits there and takes a grilling without repeatedly proclaiming their innocence. Whenever there's a lull in the interrogation, calmly and confidently insist that you're not the guilty party. Police detectives also know that the minute a suspect starts to negotiate ("What if I told you that there's a shipment coming in this Saturday?"), they've got their man.

KNOW YOUR ENEMY: VENOM

Name: Eddie Brock
First Appearance: *Amazing Spider-Man* #298 (1988)
Height and Weight: 6'3" (191 cm), 260 pounds (118 kg)
Powers: Superhuman strength, ability to stick to most surfaces, unlimited web-shooters, ability to mimic his surroundings or the appearance of other people, undetectable to Spider-Sense
Equipment: Symbiotic alien costume

Next time you complain about a lousy week at work, consider the case of Eddie Brock. As a *Daily Globe* reporter, he'd just broken the case of the murderous Sin Eater by publishing the name of a man who'd confessed. Unfortunately for Eddie, Spider-Man caught the *real* Sin-Eater shortly after. Brock (who'd been duped by a "serial confessor") was the laughingstock of the newspaper world. He was fired, disowned by his father, and divorced by his wife. But those were minor problems. He'd also recently been diagnosed with cancer and given three months to live. Eddie decided to end his misery and went to church to ask God's forgiveness. What he got was a miracle.

It came in the form of an alien symbiote that had, until recently, belonged to Spider-Man. The web-slinger had broken free of the living costume by standing in the church's bell tower and subjecting the costume to deafening noise. After hiding in the church, the alien merged with the despondent Brock, infusing him with Spidey's powers (and then some) and transforming him into a giant fanged nightmare that took the name Venom. Why Eddie? Maybe because his cancer produced high levels of adrenaline, which the symbiote draws power from. Or maybe because both beings had a reason to get even with Spider-Man. Either way, both Brock and the alien had new leases on life, and their first order of business was putting Spidey out of business.

That's proven a bit harder than Venom anticipated, but he's come close. While he has all of Spidey's powers (plus the ability to change his appearance and render himself invisible), he has some vulnerabilities that the web-slinger doesn't—namely a sensitivity to extreme temperatures and loud noises. Though they've battled time and time again, Venom and Spidey have also teamed up more than once (notably to fight the symbiote's "offspring," Carnage).

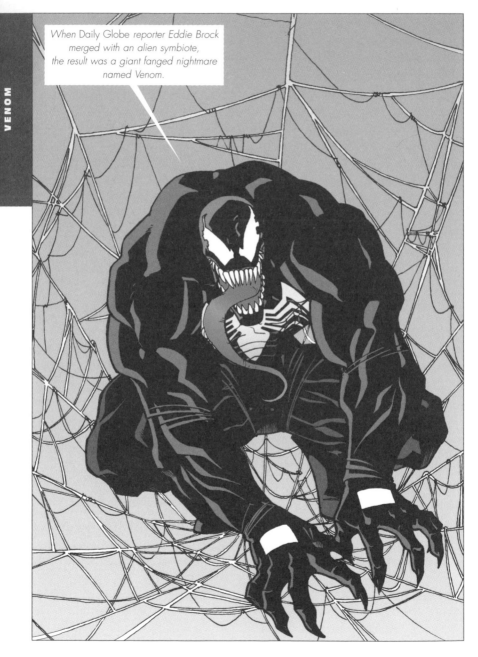

When Daily Globe reporter Eddie Brock merged with an alien symbiote, the result was a giant fanged nightmare named Venom.

VENOM

Chapter 5

Peter Parker Skills

"A hero is no braver than an ordinary man, but he is braver five minutes longer."
—Ralph Waldo Emerson

It's not always flying gliders or alien symbiotes. Sometimes, the greatest threats to Spider-Man's welfare come in the form of late notices, grouchy bosses, and unhappy spouses. Keep the city safe? Piece of cake. Keep a marriage together when you're out every night roaming the rooftops? Now *that's* a job for a super hero.

How to Deal with the Death of a Loved One

Being a super hero is the world's most dangerous job—and not just for the people wearing the tights. Spider-Man's web-slinging career was only hours old when it claimed his beloved Uncle Ben. Since then, he's attended more funerals than anyone should have to, including his first love's (see "The Women in Spider-Man's Life," page 157). According to a study commissioned by the Bureau of Super Hero Statistics, the friends and relatives of masked do-gooders are 61 times more likely to suffer tragic deaths than the general population (the majority of these can be attributed to revenge killings by the hero's enemies). So if your heart is set on going into the super hero business, enter not just at your own risk, but at the risk of everyone you care about. And while you can't protect all of them, you have to learn to protect yourself in the event of a tragedy.

Oh, and morbid as it seems, investing in a headstone company wouldn't be a half-bad idea, either.

Know the five stages of grief.

In 1969, Swiss psychiatrist Elisabeth Kübler-Ross defined the five stages of grief. And while not everyone experiences all five (or in the same order), acquainting yourself with them lets you know what to expect during your own grieving process.

1. Denial: "She can't be dead. She'll turn up, and everything will be fine."

2. Anger: "How could this happen to me? It's not fair!"

3. Bargaining: "If she comes back, I promise never to wear the costume again."

4. Depression: "The world is an ugly place full of shape-shifting villains and psychotic robots."

5. Acceptance: "Wow. She really is dead. Well . . . on to the next one."

For super heroes, there's typically an added layer of guilt—the feeling that "if only I'd been there sooner, she'd still be alive."

Don't hold back your emotions.

Super-folks tend to play it close to the chest, emotionally speaking. And while stoicism has its place (you wouldn't want to sob every time a villain tossed an insult your way), it doesn't mix well with the grieving process. Holding back the urge to cry, or scream, or pound the floor only drags things out and makes you increasingly miserable. There's no shame in breaking down and having a sniffle—no matter how tough you fancy yourself. The only shame is in being too weak to confront the pain of your loss.

Take care of your body.

Intense grief can wreak havoc on the body. Loss of appetite, stomach pain, insomnia, and headaches are all common complaints of the bereaved. Unfortunately, some people have a tendency to self-medicate these symptoms—not with aspirin or pink liquid, but with drugs and alcohol. And there's nothing more embarrassing than a drunken super hero. See your physician, who can prescribe nonaddictive sleep aids, stomach and ulcer medication, and even antidepressants to help you through the mourning period. And take care of yourself by getting plenty of food and rest.

Seek outside help if necessary.

Just as there's no shame in breaking down and crying, there's nothing wrong with seeking professional help if your loss is too overwhelming. Some people experience panic attacks, suicidal thoughts, intense anxiety, and prolonged depression as a result of a loved one's death. All are serious issues that deserve the attention of a psychiatrist. In addition to one-on-one therapy, there are bereavement groups made up of people who are going through the same thing.

THE WOMEN IN SPIDER-MAN'S LIFE

They run the gamut between old and young. Frail and acrobatic. Dead and alive. They're the women in Peter's—and Spidey's—life. Some have been romantic interests, from his first steady gal, Betty Brant, to the kooky college student, Debra Whitman. There was Liz Allen, the popular high school girl who married Pete's best friend, Harry, and Felicia Hardy (a.k.a. Black Cat), a mysterious heroine with a serious case of spider-lust. There have been allies (Silver Sable and Dagger) and enemies (Calypso and Queen). But of all the women (and super-women) in Spidey's life, these three have had the most lasting impact:

May Parker

She was the doting (some might say overprotective) aunt, the moral compass, and the only mother Peter ever knew. A kind, strong woman who rose to the challenge of raising a teenager by herself, despite a meager income and frequently poor health. After a retirement filled with countless adventures, May was finally laid to rest in *Amazing Spider-Man* #400 (1995). But don't pull out that handkerchief just yet. Subsequent issues revealed that the body belonged to an actress; Aunt May remains alive and well.

Mary-Jane Parker (Watson)

Actress, model, and redheaded wife of the one and only web-slinger. Mary-Jane's childhood (like her future husband's) was largely unhappy. She fled an abusive Pennsylvania home for New York and moved in with her aunt, next door to another young, troubled individual who—as fate would have it—also lived with his aunt. And so began the rocky courtship that would last years. Unbeknownst to Peter, MJ had learned his secret while they were still neighbors, and wouldn't date him for fear that he'd wind up dead. She even rejected Pete's first marriage proposal. But eventually, the bells tolled, the birds sang, and Spidey scored a wife—one who (famously) quipped, "Face it, tiger . . . you hit the jackpot!"

Gwen Stacy

If there's one thing nobody wants to be famous for, it's their death. But that's exactly the fate that befell (no pun intended) poor Gwen Stacy. She was a drop-dead (really, no pun at all) gorgeous girl who first met Peter when they were biochemistry students at Empire State University. Pete fell web-shooters over heels in love with the brainy blonde, even going so far as to reject the advances of his future spouse, MJ. But dating super heroes is a risky business, which Gwen learned the hard way when she was captured by the Green Goblin and taken to the top of the George Washington Bridge. Spidey took the bait, and while the two battled, Gwen was knocked over the side. Spider-Man caught her with a web strand, but it was too late . . . she was gone. The question remains—one that's plagued Spider-Fans for years: Was she already dead, or did the "snap" of being caught by Spidey's webbing kill her? Either way, her demise threw Spider-Man into a rage, and for once, he was ready to kill (see "Know Your Enemy: The Green Goblin," page 58).

How to Live on a Meager Income

Unlike many of his super hero contemporaries, Spider-Man comes from humble beginnings. He's not a billionaire business mogul like Tony Stark (Iron Man) or an "old money" heir like Charles Xavier (Professor X)—he's a lower-middle-class kid from Queens who learned to pull his own weight at an early age. Not that he had much choice—Aunt May and Uncle Ben were perpetually strapped for cash (though they always did their best to provide for the lad). And it speaks volumes to Peter's character that despite rarely having two pennies to rub together, he's still filled with humor and kindness. Of course, anyone who can see the nobility in poverty probably isn't poor. So let's cut to the chase—you're struggling, and you've just about stretched every dollar to the breaking point. Or so you think . . .

▨▨▨▨ Keep all your receipts for one week.
The first step in reigning in your spending is . . . well, knowing what you're spending money on. Pick a week, and resolve to hold on to every single receipt. If a receipt isn't available (a subway fare or vending machine, for instance) then record the transaction in a notebook. At the end of the week, sit down and go through every receipt and notebook entry, separating them into categories like:

- Groceries
- Restaurants/Fast Food/Delivery
- Entertainment (movies, books, and CDs)
- Gas/Fares

Multiply the totals for each category by four to determine your monthly totals for each category. Then, add your other monthly bills, like:

- Rent
- Car
- Insurance
  (health, life, home, and car)
- Utilities
  (gas, water, electric, and sanitation)
- Cable/Satellite
- Internet
- Credit Card Payments

When you add all the totals together, you have the magic monthly "nut"—the amount of money it takes to keep you alive each month.

████▶◀ Find the leaks in your spending.

Now that you have an accurate picture of your spending, it's time to face some cold, hard truths. Where are you wasting money? Do you watch all those channels? Is dining out four nights a week a good idea? Do you really need all those DVDs? It's time to plug some of the holes in your wallet, and who knows—maybe even save a few bucks here and there. True, many expenses are nonnegotiable—your rent or mortgage, groceries, utilities, childcare, tuition, insurance, and loan payments (credit cards, student loans, cars). But many are luxuries—restaurants, bars, concerts, movies, books (have no fear, this one was a wise investment), gadgets, music downloads, satellite, Internet, new clothes, beauty supplies, and haircuts, to name a few. If you're having trouble making ends meet, the answer lurks not in your mortgage payment, but in the murky depths of your $175 haircuts and digital music–playing toothbrushes.

████▶◀ Beware of plastic.

Credit cards aren't necessarily evil—after all, they can be handy in a pinch, and when responsibly used, they can help you build up your credit rating (which, in turn, makes it easier for you to get a loan or buy a house). But if you're the type of person who fills out every "preapproved" offer that comes in the mail, it's time to check yourself before you wreck yourself. Here are a couple of plastic pitfalls:

- A deck of cards: Having one or two cards is fine, so long as you keep the balances low and make your monthly payments on time. But if you find yourself buying a bigger wallet to accommodate your ever-growing stack, something's wrong.

- Monthly minimums: Credit card bills have a "minimum payment" figure—usually 2.5 percent of your balance. And though it's tempting to write that check and get on with your life, consider this: If you make the minimum payment on an $8,000 balance ($200) it will take you *32 and a half years* to pay it off, and you'll have spent $13,364.89 in interest. If you added just *50 bucks* a month to your payment, you'd be out of debt in less than four years and save yourself over $10,000 in interest.

Peter Parker ponders his bills, searching for "leaks" in his spending.

The typical American carries between $8,000 and $9,000 in credit card debt, with an average interest rate of 18.9 percent. That translates to more than $1,600 a year in interest alone (or $4.38 a day).

Make it at home.

If Peter spends two dollars a day on coffee, he's forking over $730 a year (throw in a cinnamon twist, and it's more like $1,500). If he spends $100 a week on restaurants, fast food, and delivery combined (an impossibly low number for most urbanites), he's out $5,200 by the end of December. But if he cuts his restaurant patronage in half (and cooks at home more often) and brews his own java every other day, he'll save $3,000 per year. In 2007 dollars, that's enough for a trip to Milan with Mary-Jane, or a brand new moped, or dinner for two at one of New York's trendier eateries.

Start an emergency fund.

Emergencies happen (especially when you're a super hero), and when you're living paycheck to paycheck, they can spell disaster for your bank account. What if your web-shooters get smashed? What if a robot assassin tears up your apartment? What if your car won't start? A smart hero plans for the worst and hopes for the best, and in this case, that means adding an "emergency fund" contribution to your monthly budget. Even if you can only spare $25 or $50 a month, that'll leave you with a $300 or $600 fund at year's end. It may sound like a pittance, but if the TV short circuits or the fridge goes on the fritz, you'll be thanking your lucky stars for that extra scratch.

Cut down on energy costs.

Energy bills can't be avoided, but they can be tamed, and without making any significant dents in your lifestyle:

- Energy-efficient transportation: City dwellers have the option of using mass transit, bikes, and (like Peter Parker) a fuel-efficient moped or scooter. But if you need a car, virtually every major automaker has a hybrid in its lineup. Depending on how much you drive and what you pay for gas, switching to a hybrid can save you hundreds of dollars a year in fuel costs.

- Energy-saving light bulbs: They cost more to buy but last up to 12 times longer (up to eight years) than standard incandescent bulbs, all while operating on less energy.

- Heat and A/C: When using the heat or air conditioning, close the doors of any rooms that aren't occupied. When you leave home in the winter, throw a blanket over the dog and turn the heat off. In the summer, close your curtains during the day to keep the sun from baking the interior.

- Appliance maintenance: Frost builds up inside refrigerators and reduces their efficiency. To make sure your ice box isn't working overtime and sucking up electricity, defrost it on a regular basis. And if you have a dryer, keep that lint screen clean.

How to Be
Where the Action Is

Chasing purse snatchers, hanging from helicopter skids, and dodging bullets are (hopefully) once-in-a-lifetime occurrences for most people. But for the average mask-wearing maven, they're as common as a stroll to the corner store. Like all top-notch good guys, Spider-Man has a knack for being in the right place at the right crime. Part of that knack can be attributed to C.A.P.E.—or "Criminal Attraction to Professional Enforcers"—the widely accepted* scientific theory that simply being a super hero vastly increases your chances of encountering crime. But a hero can't live on chance alone. As an old football coach once said, "A champion makes his own luck," and Spidey is no exception. His daily life is designed to maximize the likelihood of bumping into bad guys. After all, it's kind of hard to be a crime fighter without the crime.

Choose an action-friendly profession for your secret identity. Having a day job with flexible hours is great (see "How to Maintain a Secret Identity," page 46), but having a day job that complements your crime-fighting career is even better. Peter Parker's photojournalism keeps him out of the cubicle crucible *and* provides a handy excuse to speed off in the direction of sirens—but it doesn't necessarily invite danger. If super heroes held "alter-ego career fairs," they would place a premium on jobs that acted like magnets for dire situations and unsavory characters. Walking amongst the booths, you might see some of these types:

- Police officer: The up side: There's nothing like a badge for unfettered access to the city's most dangerous people and places. The down side: The pay scale leaves something to be desired, and sitting in a patrol car all day might not be your idea of heroic.

- Private investigator: The up side: If you're more of a loner, the old frosted glass door might be a perfect place to paint your name. The down side: You might end up following more philandering husbands than dangerous criminals.

*And completely made up.

- Investigative journalist: Specifically, one who covers the city beat for a local paper or serves as an on-camera reporter for a local news station. The up side: Better pay and access to some of the city's power players (politicians, aristocrats) that could benefit your crime-fighting efforts down the road. The down side: Having to deal with politicians and aristocrats.

- Mysterious drifter: The up side: A chance to see the world and a never-ending supply of people who need rescuing. The down side: The benefits package is lousy.

Be in the right place.

A crime fighter who lives in Chugwater, Wyoming,* isn't going to be as busy as a crime fighter who patrols the streets of Los Angeles. Whether it's Gotham, Metropolis, or New York, big super heroes need big cities. And within those cities, some neighborhoods are more deserving of attention than others. One of your super-heroic duties is staying on top of the crime statistics for your hometown. Where are the most violent crimes committed (and during what hours)? What businesses are most frequently robbed? Is there a recent wave of burglaries in a particular area?

Scan the airwaves.

Even in the worst neighborhoods, you could wander the streets all night without encountering a single crime. To maximize efficiency (and minimize wear on your soles), it helps to keep a portable scanner clipped to your utility belt. You'll be able to monitor local police and fire chatter from your favorite rooftop (or favorite sofa) and save energy for those three-alarm blazes and "calling all cars" emergencies (see "Know Your Police Codes," page 90).

Join a super hero league.

Spidey's many things, but "team player" isn't one of them. He generally doesn't work in super-groups, but he has helped them on numerous occasions, teaming up with the aforementioned Avengers, Fantastic Four, and X-Men. Group affiliation has some obvious advantages: strength in numbers, cool headquarters to lounge around in, and ten percent off at participating retailers with your membership card. It's also a great way to stay busy. If you have five teammates from different

---

*Not completely made up.

parts of the city—each with their own archvillains and ongoing sagas—chances are you'll see five times the action.

DON'T CALL US, WE'LL CALL YOU

Public service is one thing. But public servitude? Some super heroes take the convenience-store approach—whatever you need, 24 hours a day. They jump out of bed any time a signal light appears in the heavens (Spidey's dabbled in this method himself). They even take your calls—the Avengers and Fantastic Four both have hotlines where any John Q. can leave a voicemail, like "my brother's being mean to me," or "there seems to be a gateway to another dimension in my oven." Daredevil's been known to carry a pager (how did he read the numbers?), and Ghost Rider is mysteriously drawn toward any evil in his vicinity (insert your own lawyer/agent/ex-wife joke here). But the X-Men have it worst of all: Any time Charles Xavier wants to gather his flock, he merely sends an e-mail to their *thoughts*. There's no "sorry, didn't get your message" excuse for the uncanny mutants.

Do yourself (and the people you protect) a favor: Take some time off to live your life. Forget the two-way wristwatches, the red phone in the mayor's office, and the coin-operated spotlight. You're a shining beacon of justice, not a butler.

How to Deal with a Nightmare Boss

Spider-Man has vanquished all manner of man and beast over the course of his super-career. He's survived alternate universes, voodoo curses, and heartbreaking losses. And yet there's one thing that still strikes dread into his oversized heart . . . J. Jonah Jameson.

He's the publisher of the *Daily Bugle* and personification of every negative boss stereotype in the book. Spidey has two reasons to loathe the silver-streaked cigar hound. When he's in Peter Parker mode, Jameson is his egotistical, abrasive, penny-pinching boss. When Peter becomes Spider-Man, Jameson is the super hero's most vocal (and powerful) critic, constantly trying to portray the web-slinger as a menace on the *Bugle's* front page. And though it might be deeply satisfying to toss him off the Empire State Building, 1) Pete would be out of a job, and 2) that's not how Spidey handles his business. As a wise old man once said, "There are alternatives to fighting." If you find yourself losing more sleep over a supervisor than a super-villain, use the following list of manager types to identify (and ultimately outsmart) your boss.

The micromanager

He needs to have a hand in every decision, great and small, and believes he's better at everyone's job than they are. But that level of distrust can be a double-edged sword:

- Beat him at his own game: Copy him on every e-mail, memo, fax, letter, and report that you can get your mitts on. Invite him to every meeting, and drop by his office with hourly updates (if there's nothing to report, give him a breakdown of the flavored creamers available in the kitchenette).

- Cater to his ego: Constantly ask his for his input. Pull him out of a meeting to ask him what color highlighter you should use. Call him at home to get his take on the appropriate size of paperclips. When he gives an answer, blame your own stupidity for not seeing it so clearly in the first place.

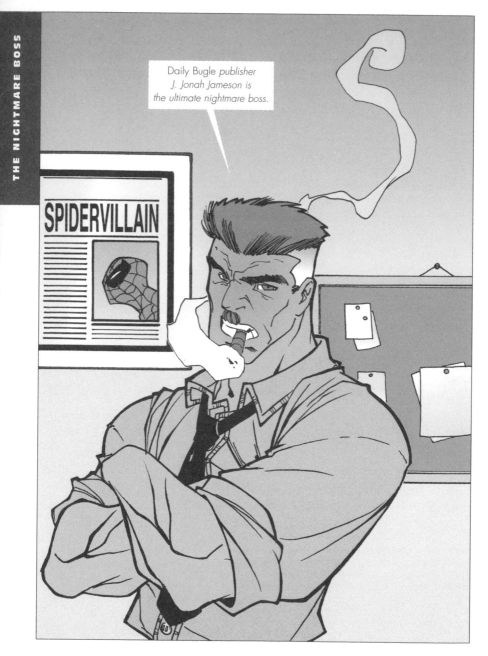

The panicmonger

"Why aren't you stressing out? The fact that you're not stressing out is stressing me out! Do you understand how stressful this job is? Do you? Because you're not acting like you do!"

- Point her thoughts away from the office: Talk about family, current events (so long as they don't pertain to work), the bond market, celebrity gossip, medical curiosities, the unbearable cuteness of baby pandas—*anything* to remind her that there are other things going in the world.

- Feign hyperobsessive dedication: Come in a little more disheveled every day (this may not require too much acting if you've had a busy night of super-heroics). Leave your desk littered with empty coffee cups and caffeine pills, and keep your head buried in stacks of papers when you walk the halls. If someone asks how you are, say, "I don't see how that's relevant to the company."

The screamer

Make a mistake, and you're an "idiot." Move too slow, and you're "stealing money." Like many of your alter ego's enemies, screaming bosses thrive on threats, put-downs, and intimidation, and prefer to deliver them at the top of their voice. Luckily, there's a surefire countermeasure:

- Send signals of a dangerous imbalance: Keep family photos on your desk, but cut out all the eyes. If he comments on the missing eyes, insist that they're still there. Bring every conversation back to taxidermy. If he says, "There's nothing like a weekend of golfing," say, "Yes there is—a weekend of taxidermy." Ask him why he hired a little girl. When he asks, "What little girl?" point near him and say, "The one standing right there."

The friend

Anyone who works for J. J. Jameson needn't worry about this one. But a boss who wants to be your buddy can be worse than any screamer, panicmonger, or micromanager. Why? Because if she succeeds, you wind up with a seven-day-a-week attachment to the office.

- Avoid discussing your personal life: Just as you don't want Hannibal Lecter rooting around in your skull, you can't afford to give her any mental real estate.

She'll recount every detail of her childhood, love life, and weekend activities, and ask you to do the same. Don't. Deflect the conversation away from yourself by asking more questions about her life. If she persists, be as vague as possible.

- "Oh, you can't make it? That's too bad": Offer up invitations to social events only when you're absolutely sure she can't make it.

THREE TIPS FOR TAKING DECENT PICTURES

Peter tries to stay off J. J. Jameson's bad side (it only takes up one side?) by delivering snappy snapshots of Spidey. And though Pete never went to school for photography, his teenaged eye was good enough to earn a full-time job at New York's biggest newspaper. Here are a few tips he uses to get great shots.

- **Thirds:** Think of the frame as a tic-tac-toe board—three horizontal sections and three vertical sections. For more interesting shots, try placing your subject off center—the left or right third when shooting horizontally, or the top or bottom third when shooting vertically.

- **Eye level:** When shooting human subjects, placing the camera at eye level usually makes for a better snap.

- **Separation:** To make the subject stand out, place it in a neutral, uncluttered setting, and use longer lenses to keep distracting background details out of focus. When shooting humans, light them from behind to give their head and shoulders an edge.

How to Stay Married to an Actress

Making a marriage work is hard enough. But when your spouse is an actress (or worse, a famous actress) you might as well hold your wedding reception in a divorce attorney's lobby. Fame is the ultimate home wrecker, whether the celeb-betrothed is male or female, movie star or sports idol. And while Peter and Mary-Jane have beaten the curse thus far, it hasn't been picture-perfect. There have been fits of jealously, invasions of privacy—even a trial separation. Sure, it's true love. Sure, it's fate. But those aren't enough. Not when your wife's mug is plastered on the tabloids with rumors of a new steamy fling every other week (granted, being married to a super hero's no cup of tea, either, but that's another book). If this is gonna last, you'll need an emergency ego-ectomy and a maturity transfusion, stat.

Don't tie your self-worth to your net worth.
Peter Parker may be an exceptional super hero specimen, but he's also an ordinary guy. He wants to be the provider. The breadwinner. And he's struggled with being a distant second in the income department, especially when he's found himself unemployed. But the disparity (no matter how great) between your earning power and your wife's has nothing to do with how she or anyone else actually perceives you, and obsessing over it is merely a product of your insecurity. Instead of being jealous, why not relish the fact that you can get the best tables without a reservation? Why not build that ship in a bottle you've been putting off? Why not buy yourself something nice? On second thought, why not get *her* something nice? After all, she's buying.

Don't get her name tattooed on your arm next to the word "forever," carry a vial of her blood, or jump up and down like a maniac proclaiming your undying love on talk shows.
Doing any of these things virtually guarantees the relationship will crash and burn inside of six months.

Don't believe everything you read.

Once, Mary-Jane was photographed entering Stark Towers, fueling a newspaper story that she and Tony Stark (Iron Man) were having an affair. Now, if Spidey had taken the story at face value, we'd have likely witnessed one of the great "you were supposed to be my friend!" fistfights of all time. Luckily, the web-slinger had 1) more sense than that, and 2) more faith in his wife than that. Which leads us to . . .

Don't be possessive.

MJ's had some dashing leading men, especially during her soap opera days. More recently, when she landed a role in a Hollywood super hero movie (starring the amazing "Lobster-Man!") Peter had to twiddle his thumbs while various Hollywood slimeballs put the moves on his wife. With all those vultures circling overhead, most men would be terrified to let her out of their sight. But playing the jealous type gets you nowhere. Just keep reminding yourself that even though you're not as wealthy, funny, or handsome as the men she's chatting with, she's still going home with you at the end of the night. (If she *doesn't*, then yes, you might have a problem).

Finally, remember to be a loving, faithful, and attentive husband.

Because no matter how many tons you can lift or walls you can cling to, she still has the power to send you somewhere far more terrifying than any alternate universe or secret lair: the pull-out sofa.

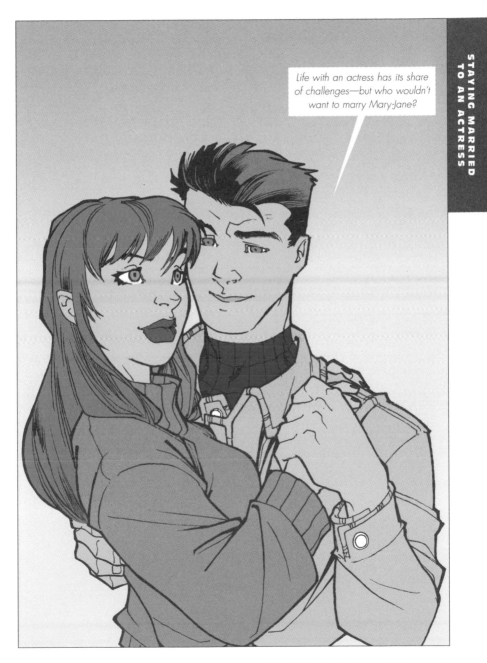

Life with an actress has its share of challenges—but who wouldn't want to marry Mary-Jane?

Acknowledgments

Thanks to all my friends in Quirk's top-secret headquarters: Mike Rogalski, Kevin Kosbab, Melissa Monachello, and David Borgenicht. And as always, a special thanks to Jason Rekulak, my very own (young, male, and unrelated) Aunt May. I'm also grateful to comic book artist Carlo Barberi, who brought an abundance of wit and imagination to this book's illustrations.

I would've been doomed without my trusty "Spider-Squad"—a small band of web-headed misfits who provided expert knowledge, suggestions, feedback, and enthusiasm. From SpiderFan.org: Steve Christensen, Gabriel Shechter, Henrique Ferreira, Robert J. Sodaro, Paul Sebert, Max Lacey, Stan Szewczyk, and Craig Lowrey. From my own backyard: the fanboy-tastic duo of Brent Simons and Eric Goldman. And above all, Jason Smith, whose speedy replies and epic knowledge always seemed (like Spidey) to save my neck in the nick of time.

And finally, to Stan Lee and Steve Ditko—thanks for everything.

About the Spider-Crew

Seth Grahame-Smith protects the streets of Los Angeles with his super hero wife, Erin, and their dog, Logan—who has no powers whatsoever.

Carlo Barberi began illustrating comic books eight years ago with Dark Horse, and his adaptable style has kept him in demand. He came to Marvel as an artist for the New Mutants series, and he currently pencils for the *Justice League Unlimited* animated series. He lives in Monterrey, Mexico.

Stan "The Man" Lee is the cocreator of Spider-Man, the Incredible Hulk, X-Men, the Fantastic Four, and countless other comic book characters. More than two billion of his comic books have been published in 75 countries and 25 languages. He is the chairman emeritus of Marvel Enterprises, Inc.